Library of
Davidson College

ANCIENT PHILOSOPHY

Editions
Commentaries
Critical Works

Edited by
LEONARDO TARAN
Columbia University

A Garland Series

GRACE HADLEY BILLINGS

THE ART OF TRANSITION IN PLATO

GARLAND PUBLISHING, INC.
NEW YORK & LONDON
1979

*For a complete list of the titles in this series,
see the final pages of this volume.*

The volumes in this series are printed on acid-free,
250-year-life paper.

Bibliographical note:
This facsimile has been made from a copy in
the Yale University Library (Gfp66.y920).

Library of Congress Cataloging in Publication Data

Billings, Grace Elvina Hadley, Mrs.
  The art of transition in Plato.

  (Ancient philosophy ; 2)
  Reprint of the 1920 ed. published by G. Banta Pub.
Co., Menasha, Wis., originally presented as the
author's thesis, University of Chicago.
  1. Plato—Style. 2. Plato—Technique. I. Title.
  II. Series.
  PA4329.B5 1979   184   78-66578
          ISBN 0-8240-9609-6

Printed in the United States of America

The University of Chicago

The Art of Transition in Plato

A DISSERTATION
SUBMITTED TO THE FACULTY OF THE GRADUATE SCHOOL OF ARTS
AND LITERATURE IN CANDIDACY FOR THE DEGREE
OF DOCTOR OF PHILOSOPHY
DEPARTMENT OF GREEK

BY
GRACE HADLEY BILLINGS

A Private Edition, Distributed By
THE UNIVERSITY OF CHICAGO LIBRARIES
CHICAGO, ILLINOIS
1920

The Collegiate Press
GEORGE BANTA PUBLISHING COMPANY
MENASHA, WISCONSIN

TABLE OF CONTENTS

                                                                PAGE
Introduction...   1

Chapter
  I. MAIN TRANSITIONS....................................   4
       The dramatic introduction—Transition from the introduction to the main body of the dialogue—The dramatic conclusion—Transition from the main body of the dialogue to the conclusion—Transitions between larger subdivisions in the main body of the dialogue; brief analysis in case of the Laches, Gorgias, Phaedrus, Meno; detailed analysis of Phaedo, Theaetetus, Philebus, Republic, Laws.

  II. MINOR CONVENTIONAL FORMS OF TRANSITION............. 53
       Transition by explicit reference to the plan and course of the argument—Cross reference—Dismissive introductive forms—Formulas of omission or postponement—Dismissive and summarizing transitions—Transition by assumption—Dichotomy in transition—Transition by new suggestion—Introduction of new terms—Transition by definition—Transition by criticism or correction—The shift from general to particular and vice versa—Applied analogous illustrations—Enumerations—Inferential particles—Interrogative formulas—Transitional adverb and prepositional phrases—Connective particles—Narrative formulas.

  III. THE LITERARY ART OF TRANSITION.................... 71
       Introductory—Examples of artistic transitions—Plato's transitional usage of proverbs, quotations, images, continued metaphor, leit motif—Word transitions—Various literary methods of advancing the argument—Playing with the order of the subject—Blending of literary devices with real argument—Digressions—Parodies.

APPENDIX... 102

PREFACE

The following study of Plato's methods of transition was undertaken at the suggestion of Professor Paul Shorey of the University of Chicago. My warm thanks are due to him for his invaluable help and criticism during the progress of the work. Former members of his seminar on Plato will find my indebtedness to Professor Shorey especially evident in the section on the *Republic*. I am sorry that his long-promised edition of the *Republic* is not yet in print so that my acknowledgment might be more definite. I wish also to express here my thanks to Dr. Thomas H. Billings of Carleton College and Miss Frances W. Hadley who have generously borne the entire burden of the proof-reading.

GRACE HADLEY BILLINGS.

Northfield, Minnesota,
August, 1920.

THE ART OF TRANSITION IN PLATO

INTRODUCTION

The subject of the methods of transition used by Greek and Latin writers has by no means received the attention it deserves.[1] The value of such a study for the understanding and appreciation of an author's style is readily apparent. Nor is the investigation so simple as it might at first sight appear. The elusiveness of the subject and its difficulties will be illustrated in the following paper. The inquiry has been confined to the Platonic dialogues.[2] Our first problem is one of method. Platonic thought seems to follow whither the wind blows;[3] in reality it is guided by a subtle art. A study of the process might develop into a treatise on Platonic dialectic, on the logic of Plato's style. This would necessitate a complete analysis of the argument of every dialogue, showing Plato's logical methods of thought-transition. Moreover, in the dialogues, while the stream of thought is continuous, yet it runs from point to point. Every sentence is connected, explicitly or implicitly, with what precedes and follows. A study of transitions might become an attempt to classify all the forms of sentence connection.[4] This latter interpretation of the subject involves another. Its constant use of particles is a prominent idiomatic characteristic of the Greek language. Many particles are distinctly particles of connection, and most of them have

[1] Two recent Yale dissertations—A. R. Brubacher, *Sentence Connection in Herodotus*, New Haven, 1902, and C. W. Mendell, *Sentence Connection in Tacitus*, New Haven, 1901, approach the subject from the standpoint of historical syntax. Dr. Mendell has since published *Latin Sentence Connection*, New Haven, 1917, in which he continues his investigations in a wider field. There are also several German dissertations dealing with the mechanical formulas and phrases of transition used by the Greek orators. (Cf. p. 53, n. 1.)

[2] For a detailed survey of transitional usage in another special field, see R. D. Elliott, *Transition in the Attic Orators*, Menasha, Wis., 1919.

[3] Rep. 394d; Theaet. 172d; Laws 667a. Jowett and Campbell, *Republic of Plato*, Oxford, 1894, Vol. II, p. 10; Shorey, *Unity of Plato's Thought*, Chicago, 1903, p. 5.

[4] Dr. Mendell finds three fundamental principles underlying all sentence connection:—repetition, change and incompleteness.

some transitional usages. Thus it becomes possible to regard an account of Plato's methods of transition as practically equivalent to a treatise on Platonic particles.

The versatility of Plato's genius is responsible for a further complication of the subject. Plato's style has been aptly called panharmonic. He passes at will from simplicity to complexity, from the commonplace to impassioned eloquence without disturbing the harmony of the whole. Campbell[5] has distinguished five varieties of Platonic manner—simple statement or narration, ornate narration, passages of moral elevation, question and answer, continuous dialectic. Such a stylistic classification might be adopted as the framework for a discussion of transitions, for different methods are necessarily characteristic of each style.

The method followed in the present paper is one of compromise. Without attempting an exhaustive study of the process of Platonic dialectic, of Plato's methods of sentence connection, or his use of particles, it is the purpose of this discussion to present from the Platonic dialogues adequate material for the illustration of all these methods of approach to the study of transitions. The stylistic basis of arrangement has not been adopted, but changes in transitional method due to differences in style have been noted. The first chapter contains analyses of a number of representative dialogues. In these analyses only so much of the philosophic content of the argument is given as is necessary to make intelligible the outline of the logical and artistic framework of the dialogue. The chief emphasis is placed on the indication and description of the main points of transition in the argument. The two succeeding chapters are devoted to a more minute study of Plato's methods of transition. The second chapter deals with his usage of conventional transitional formulas and includes a brief, incomplete account of Platonic transitional particles. Under the heading 'Plato's literary art of transition' more unusual and artistic means of connection have been discussed. Little or no attempt at formal classification has been made. Similar transitional devices are grouped together for purposes of description. The frequent union of several transitional elements in one passage and the difficulty of fixing hard and fast boundaries between different types of transition make any rigid classification impossible as well as useless.

[5] Jowett and Campbell, *Republic of Plato*, Oxford, 1894, Vol. II, p. 166 ff.

The present paper, therefore, disregards most of the commonly suggested lines of division, such as the separation of transitions into personal and impersonal, explicit and disguised, natural and manufactured. Even the important distinction between an external form of connection by formula, phrase, particle, or repeated word and an inner thought-transition by means of summary, generalization, dismissal, criticism, or description of plan, has been rejected as a basis of classification. Most transitions indeed contain both an external and internal element. This discussion is occupied with the recognition and description of these as they appear in different combinations, rather than with any attempt to decide in individual passages upon which transitional element the balance of emphasis rests.

CHAPTER I

Main Transitions

Plato has no special methods which he reserves for main transitions. The device which opens a whole discussion may appear later on in a very minor subdivision. Generalizations as to the intrinsic importance of this or that transitional device are practically worthless. But a careful analysis of the main transitions in individual dialogues is by no means barren of result. It is possible to penetrate, if ever so little, the secret of that wonderful smooth style[1] where thought follows thought in a sequence so genuine that it is often hard to put one's finger on any line of division;—so completely is the whole discourse a unit.

To connect the main body of thought successfully with the introduction, so as not to leave the transition abrupt or arbitrary, is recognized by rhetoricians[2] as one of the hardest of the writer's tasks. In dealing with this difficult transitional problem Plato is pre-eminently successful. His introductions are varied and interesting. We miss the stereotyped personal proemium common in the orators.[3] An approach to the formal prothetic introduction is found in some of the later dialogues, but even there the semblance of a dramatic setting is often preserved. The Cratylus affords a good example of this type. It opens with the invitation to Socrates to join in the discussion whose theme Hermogenes briefly explains. With the usual[4] protest of ignorance from Socrates and of his willingness to investigate the subject in company with the others (384c), the argument begins. The Sophist is nearly as abrupt. After the bare men-

---

[1] Olympiodorus in his scholia to Plato's Phaedo has noted this smoothness of transition. Finckh, *Olympiodorus, Scholia in Platonis Phaedonem*, Heilbronn, 1847, p. 13 — ἀψοφητὶ τῆς μεταβάσεως γενομένης δίκην ἐλαίου ῥέοντος· οὐ γὰρ λογογραφικὸν τὸ διαιρεῖν εἰς πρῶτον καὶ δεύτερον κεφάλαιον. The figure of the stream of oil is Platonic. Cp. Theaet. 144 B.

[2] Genung, *Practical Rhetoric*, p. 283.

[3] Isoc. XII, VI; Lysias III, XII, XVI et al.; Andocides I; Aeschines II; Ant. V.

[4] Laches 186 c, Theaet. 145 e, 157 cd, Meno 71 b, 80 d, Rep. 331 e, 354 c, 450 e-451 ab, Lysis 212 a, Gorg. 506 a.

tion of the appointed meeting and a half-playful reference to the god-like character of the philosopher stranger, Socrates propounds the question for investigation. A few details of procedure are arranged and the discussion begins with the application of the chosen method to a simple subject. In several other dialogues, notably the Philebus, Parmenides, Politicus and Meno[5] the discussion begins abruptly with no dramatic preface.

Abruptness of beginning is characteristic also of the spurious dialogues.[6] The subject of discussion may be introduced entirely without prelude as in the De Justo which begins, "Can you tell us what justice is?" (372a) Where there is any attempt at a dramatic introduction it is purely conventional. The Theages will serve as a good example of this type.[7] After a few stereotyped details of place and occasion Demodocus reveals his reason for consulting Socrates;— he is worried about the education of his son. The transition to the following discourse is brought about through the common[8] Socratic principle of the need of agreement as to the meaning of the subject under discussion. (122b-e)

In the majority of the genuine dialogues a dramatic introduction, often lengthy and elaborate, prepares the way for the discussion. The predominant feature may be a vivid description of the setting, as in the Lysis,[9] or a piece of character delineation, as in the

[5] This lack of dramatic introduction natural enough in the metaphysical dialogues is noteworthy in the Meno, which is a minor dialogue of search otherwise rich in dramatic interest and clever character portrayal.

[6] Compare the De Virtute (376a) the Demodocus (380a) and the Hipparchus (225a).

[7] The Sisyphus, Eryxias and Axiochus are similarly abrupt and conventional in their introductions. Grote, *Plato*, Vol. II, p. 94, has noted that some of the genuine dialogues begin abruptly and bases upon this argument his acceptance also of some usually regarded as spurious. But among the genuine dialogues, if we except the Meno, it is the abstruse metaphysical type which is lacking in dramatic introduction. The spurious dialogues are more akin in subject matter to the minor dialogues.

[8] See Theaet. 154de; Meno 75d.

[9] In the introduction to the Lysis Socrates describes how, while walking from the Academy to the Lyceum, he met and joined a group of his young friends who were on their way to a neighboring palaestra. In their conversation on the road the subject of friendship, the dominant idea of the dialogue, is readily introduced through the criticism of Hippothales for the foolish and extravagant manner in which he addresses his friend Lysis. Socrates convinces Hippothales that he

Euthyphro;[10] or both elements may be equally important, as in the artistically perfect Protagoras. In any case these opening scenes strike the key-note of the dialogue. They forewarn us of the tone and character of the discussion which they introduce.

The dramatic introduction in the Laches is particularly appropriate, for an inquiry into the nature of courage is easily developed from a discussion of the advisability of learning the art of fighting in heavy armor.[11] The series of transitions, leading up to the main inquiry is a good illustration of Socrates' skill in guiding a conversation.[12] In the first half of the introduction Socrates has little active

ought to change and offers to advise him if he can have an opportunity to talk with Lysis. Thus transition is made to the idea of a discussion (206 c). There follows a charming description of the scene in the palaestra. Lysis and his friend Menexenus come over and sit down by Socrates and he begins to talk with them (207b).

The introduction to the Charmides is equally rich in descriptive detail.

[10] There is very little description of the setting in the Euthyphro. Socrates and Euthyphro meet in the porch of the King Archon. Both are involved in law-suits. Socrates has been charged with impiety. Euthyphro is engaged in the prosecution of his own father for the murder of a hired laborer. In the course of their conversation the question of the piety of Euthyphro's act naturally arises (4e). Socrates is eager to learn from Euthyphro what piety is in order that he may defend himself against Meletus. Thus the idea of a discussion is introduced (5c). The formal request for a definition of piety (5d) serves as the final transition to the main discourse. It is in keeping with the ironical tone which pervades the whole dialogue that the great moral teacher Socrates should be represented as anxious to become the pupil of the wrong-headed bigot Euthyphro.

[11] Equally appropriate is the choice of the two brave generals as Socrates' respondents in this discussion. Artistic selection of the characters to fit the discourse is typical of the minor dialogues. Lysis and Menexenus are an example of friendship. The youth Charmides is an embodiment of the virtue temperance. So too in the Theaet. which in many details resembles the minor dialogues the characters are adapted to their theme.

[12] The subject of the discussion is frequently introduced through Socrates' clever manipulation of the conversation. So in the Phaedo, where the final transition to the theme of the discourse, the true philosopher's willingness to die, is made through explanation of Socrates' intentionally paradoxical reply to a question of Cebes, 61 B, "Tell this, then, to Evenus, Cebes, and bid him if he be wise to follow me as quickly as possible." In the Symposium, although the narrative introduction is occupied mainly with the personality of Socrates, his lively conversation with Aristodemus on the road, his characteristic lapse into a brown study, his rallying reply to the playful admiration of Agathon's welcome, it is through the proposal of Eryximachus, 176 e f., that the subject of discourse is introduced. Socrates, however, sanctions the plan. 177 de.

part. He excuses himself modestly on the ground that he is younger and less experienced than the two generals. The long set speeches of Nicias and Laches for and against the practice under discussion form an interesting contrast to the Socratic dialogue which follows, to which transition is made by the call upon Socrates to cast the deciding vote (184d). The familiar[13] Socratic doctrine of the necessity of dependence not upon the opinion of the majority, but of the 'one wise man' forms the next onward step in transition (184e). The attempt to answer the question 'wise in what?'—to define the main point at issue—leads to the generalized distinction between means and end (185d), and by application of this distinction Socrates makes the important transition from body to soul[14] (185e). There now follows a discussion of the two tests of the claim to knowledge, ability to name one's teachers or to show some practical results of one's teaching of others. Socrates as often[15] professes ignorance (186c) in order to bring on a discussion. Lysimachus asks Nicias and Laches whether they are willing to submit to examination. The following passage, 187c–189b, with its comment upon the character of Socrates may seem like a digression, but it is important for the appreciation of the dialogue that Socrates be recognized as a moral teacher with more than a mere intellectual interest in the discussion.[16] Furthermore, the figure of the Doric harmony here introduced appears later on (193e), with unifying effect.[17] The excuse of forgetfulness by Lysimachus (189c) makes Socrates the leader of the discussion. But Socrates, when thus in control of the situation, makes a sudden

[13] Theaet. 144e; Crito 44cd.
[14] Compare Protag. 352ab; Theaet. 145ab. In Char. 154de the transition from body to soul is very cleverly managed. Socrates picks up the word ἀποδῦναι which had been used in comment on the physical beauty of Charmides and applies it to the investigation of his soul, thus giving a moral turn to the discourse.
[15] See above, p. 4, note 4.
[16] Similar in purpose is the passage in Char. 156a–157a, where the pretext of giving Charmides a remedy for the headache is used by Socrates as the occasion for a short discourse on the art of medicine and the relation between soul and body. The ethical application of these remarks leads to the question whether Charmides possesses the virtue of temperance and the lad's modesty necessitates the usual Socratic conclusion—we must investigate together.
[17] Similarly in the Euthyphro the impending trial of Socrates, which is brought into prominence in the introduction, appears as a leit-motif throughout the dialogue. See below pp. 80 and 85.

shift of the plan of inquiry to one based rather on first principles and introduces the doctrine of παρουσία[18] (189e) which he explains by a concrete illustration. This is a question of the παρουσία of virtue. Transition to discussion is made through the assumption that what we know, we must be able to express.[19] Inquiry into the nature of virtue is evaded here by the assumption that virtue is a whole with parts and the final narrowing of the question to the investigation 'what is courage?' is made by reference back to the art of fighting in heavy armor, the practice of which is supposed to produce courage.[20]

There may be debate about the extent of the dramatic introduction in the Crito. If it is regarded as including only the brief preliminary conversation, Socrates' vision with its beautiful and pathetic adaptation of the Homeric quotation, "On the third day thou shalt go to fertile Phthia" (44b), supplies the link of transition to Crito's plea that Socrates will allow his friends to plan his escape. If on the other hand, the main theme of the dialogue is not the plea for escape, but the consideration of the question whether escape is right, then Crito's arguments for the escape and the preliminary discussion of the value of the opinion of the many are to be included in the introduction, from which transition is made through the application of general principles to the particular question, and the common[21] Socratic formula, 'We must consider together.'

[18] παρουσία, presence, is one of the terms used by Plato to express the relation of the idea to the particular object. Socrates' use of the term in this passage is rather logical than metaphysical. Compare also Char. 158e–159a.

[19] A similar combination of ideas is used in Char. 158e–159a. Here it is a question of the παρουσία of temperance. The assumption that if Charmides possesses the virtue he can give an account of it introduces the demand for a definition of temperance and the beginning of the discussion.

[20] The introduction of the Laches has been criticized as disproportionate in length to the main discussion. Bonitz (Platonische Studien, Berlin, 1886, p. 226), defends Plato by the argument that it is no longer in our power to discover what special purpose he may have had in any chosen mode of expression. This seems an adequate defense. Why should not the raising of the question of the profit of professional training and the resulting typical speeches of Nicias and Laches be accepted as important to Plato's design in the Laches as well as the lessons in logic and ethics which are dramatically taught in the later discussion?

[21] Meno 80d, 81e, 86c; Theaet. 145d, 151e; Char. 158d; Crat. 384c; Laches 201a.

The introduction to the Phaedrus is rich both in descriptive detail and character delineation. Socrates meets the young Phaedrus, an enthusiastic lover of discourse, on his way for a walk outside the walls. He has just come from a visit with Lysias where he has heard a discourse on love which urged favoring the non-lover rather than the lover. Socrates begs him to repeat it. After considerable protest and feigned reluctance on the part of Phaedrus, Socrates' playful insistence is rewarded. Phaedrus admits the possession of the manuscript and suggests (228de) that they sit down and read it. The following account of their walk along the Ilissus, the interesting mythological digression suggested by the place, and the description of the fair retreat beneath the lofty plane tree are deservedly famous. Finally with some jesting by-play on Socrates' fondness for the city and the manner of his allurement to this unaccustomed distance from it, return is made to the manuscript. A resumptive δ' οὖν dismisses the by-play and with a simple ἄκουε δή the speech of Lysias is introduced.

The dialogues just discussed are of the direct dramatic type.[22] Their introductions are generally short,[23] noteworthy for character portrayal rather than scenic elaboration.[24] In the narrated dialogues[25] the introduction may include in dramatic form the request for the narrative and some preliminary conversation as well as the

[22] So also the Gorgias, Euthyphro, Laws, Ion, Menexenus, Hippias II and the doubtful Hippias I and Alc. I and II.
[23] The Laches is a notable exception.
[24] In the Gorgias the setting is not even mentioned, merely implied. The rhetorician Gorgias has just been giving an exhibition, apparently in a public hall, for which Socrates and his pupil Chaerophon have arrived too late. But what Socrates really wants is a chance to talk with Gorgias and at his request Chaerephon is on the point of asking the rhetorician to define his profession (447b) when Polus, Gorgias' pupil, interrupts and offers himself as respondent with the excuse that his master is tired. In the following conversation Chaerephon and Polus illustrate very amusingly the characteristic and contrasting styles of their respective masters. Socrates interrupts to correct Polus and draw the distinction between praise and definition. Through this lesson in elementary logic transition is made (448e) to the discussion with Gorgias, from whom Socrates now demands (449a), "But rather, Gorgias, do you tell us yourself what we ought to call you, and what is the art in which you are skilled."
[25] These include the Lysis, Charm., Protag., Phaedo, Symp., **Theaet.,** **Euthydemus,** Republic.

narrative introduction to the discussion, or, as in the Lysis and Charmides, the request may be presupposed[26] and the narrative introduction begin at once.

The brilliant and complicated Protagoras is a narrated dialogue within a dialogue and has therefore a double introduction. In the brief preliminary conversation between Socrates and an unnamed friend, the character of Alcibiades serves as the connecting link which binds this introduction to the main dialogue. Socrates turns the reference to his favorite to introduce the name of the stranger from Abdera by whose wonderful wisdom he has been so charmed that he even forgot the presence of Alcibiades the Fair. Thence the request for an account of his conversation with Protagoras follows as a matter of course (310a).

In the narrative itself our decision as to the limit of the dramatic introduction depends upon our decision as to the main purpose of the dialogue. If that is the discussion of the question whether virtue is one or many then the dramatic introduction extends through the myth of Protagoras. The method of transition at this point is a familiar one.[27] Socrates expresses great admiration for the words of the Sophist. He will feel quite satisfied if only Protagoras can clear up one little difficulty. Is virtue one and are justice, temperance and piety parts of it, or are these all names of the same thing which is one? (328e–329c)

Since however this discussion really occupies a comparatively small part of the dialogue it seems more reasonable to adopt the view that the main aim of the Protagoras is more general, the dramatic illustration of the contrast between Socratic and Sophistic methods and the superiority of dialectic. It is easy to see how the myth of

[26] In the Lysis, Charmides and Republic, Socrates is the narrator; his auditor is not even mentioned. In the Symposium, the request of the auditor, an unnamed friend, for an account of the discourse on Love at Agathon's banquet is presupposed. But since the narrative is preceded by a brief conversation between the auditor and narrator this dialogue should be classed with the Protagoras, rather than with the Lysis.

[27] Theaet. 145d, 161c, 202d; Laches 180b; Euthyph. 12e–13a, 7a; Protag. 319a, b. Cp. also below pp. 89 ff. In Char. 154de this common transitional device—the expression of satisfaction with his own or another's conclusions or ideas if only one slight addition or correction be made—is used, together with the transition from body to soul, to introduce the idea of conversation with Charmides.

Protagoras, Socrates' clever ironical parody of current methods of literary interpretation, the long dramatic interlude in which Prodicus, Hippias and the other personages of the dialogue play characteristic parts, and the several passages of actual dialectic all contribute to this general aim and unite into a complete artistic whole. Upon this view, the dramatic introduction extends to the myth of Protagoras which is then the first main division[28] of the dialogue to which transition is made through Socrates' request for clearer proof of the possibility of virtue being taught.[29]

The Euthydemus, like the Protagoras, is a narrated dialogue, but the enclosing frame is, in this case, a much more integral part of the structure, for Crito, who appears in the introduction begging Socrates for a description of his encounter with the two strangers (271a), enters also into the discussion in the midst of the narrative (290e–293a), and the dialogue closes with the consideration of the criticism of the Sophists and of Socrates which Crito has heard from a bystander, a clever writer of speeches for the courts (304c, d). His character then is a much more important unifying element than that of Alcibiades in the Protagoras.[30] In the preliminary conversation with Crito and in the narrative introduction the keynote of the whole dialogue is struck in the extravagant ironical praise which Socrates showers upon the two Sophists. The main purpose of the dialogue—the caricature and exposure of eristic methods—is clearly indicated. As in the Protagoras the question of the education and improvement of an intelligent youth furnishes the excuse for the ensuing discussion. Socrates urges the Sophists (275a) to postpone until another time their display of other matters, but for the present to persuade Cleinias that he ought to study philosophy and practise virtue. This they

---

[28] For description of the transitions between the other four important subdivisions of the dialogue see below p. 17, notes 50 and 51 and p. 58, n. 33.

[29] Or the introduction may be considered as extending only to 318a where, after the decision for a public discussion and the description of the grouping of the audience, Socrates puts for a second time the question, 'What will happen to the youth Hippocrates if he associates with Protagoras?'

[30] Similarly in the Phaedo Echecrates is more than a mere deus ex machina whose formal request is the occasion of the narrative. Twice during the dialogue (88c and 102a) some comment of his to Phaedo upon the narrative marks a crisis in the argument and his name appears also at the very end. He is a real, sympathetic auditor of whose presence we are kept conscious throughout.

agree to do if the youth will only answer. He is used to that, says Socrates; and so the fun begins.

Although the Theaetetus is a dialogue within a dialogue it differs from the others of that class. The discussion is not narrated, but is presented as a written manuscript giving in true dialogue form the exact words of each speaker,[31] and thus avoiding the constant repetition of "said he" and "said I." The recollection and mention of the discussion is occasioned very naturally by the fact that Euclides has just been escorting the sick and wounded Theaetetus on his way from Corinth to Athens. The usual[32] request to hear the tale follows. The reading of the manuscript is prefaced by explanation of its form (143c). The dramatic introduction to the dialogue proper is developed quite in the style of the minor dialogues.[33] Socrates uses the remark of Theodorus as to the personal resemblance between Theaetetus and himself (144e) to introduce the idea of the authority of the specialist. But while Theodorus is not to be trusted as to physical resemblance his praise of Theaetetus for virtue of Soul constrains the lad to submit to examination. Having thus, by means of the familiar transition from body to soul[34] (145b), introduced the idea of a discussion, Socrates begins to question Theaetetus about his studies. The transition thence to the main topic of the dialogue is easy. Socrates is himself a learner, but he has "one little difficulty"[35] (145de), which he hopes Theaetetus and the rest will help him to solve—"what is knowledge?" Theodorus excuses himself on the ground that he is inexperienced in dialectic and Theaetetus becomes the respondent (146b).

There is less variety in Plato's conclusions than in his introductions. Some endings like that of the Republic are carefully planned

[31] This plan may have been adopted for the sake of greater verisimilitude since the accurate repetition of such a long and complicated argument would be an improbable feat. So in the Symposium (178a) Plato represents Apollodorus as warning his friend just before he proceeds to recount the speech of Phaedrus that he does not himself remember exactly everything that Aristodemus told him, nor did Aristodemus remember exactly all that each one said. That in reality Plato cared little for verisimilitude in such details is evident from his disregard of time probabilities in the Republic. See p. 40, n. 132.

[32] Protag. 310a; Phaedo 57a; Euthyd. 271a.
[33] See above p. 5 f. and also p. 7, n. 16.
[34] See above p. 7 and n. 14.
[35] See above p. 10 and note 27.

for artistic climactic effect. But in general they are not so well managed as the introductions; they are more stereotyped, less effective. The Sophist has no dramatic conclusion; it ends abruptly with a summary[36] of the final definition of the sophist (268c–d) and its acceptance by Theaetetus. In the Cratylus the polemic against the flowing philosophers closes, in the style of the minor dialogues,[37] with a Socratic profession of ignorance and recommendation to further inquiry.[38] The transition to the conclusion is made by the sudden and perfunctory introduction (440e) of the common[39] formula of postponement, εἰς αὖθις τοίνυν. The Meno ends almost as abruptly as it began. After the statement of the final conclusion of the discussion (100b) Socrates makes a last protest against their order of investigation. The question what is virtue should be settled first. The formula of withdrawal νῦν δ' ἐμοὶ μὲν ὥρα ποι ἰέναι follows abruptly and the dialogue closes with a significant reference to the angry Anytus.

The dialogues just considered illustrate abrupt and rather mechanical methods of conclusion. In several of the dialogues the closing scene, though brief, is developed in a style which recalls the dramatic introduction. In the Charmides Socrates' summary[40] of the results of the inquiry (175a), which follows the rejection of the sixth defini-

---

[36] The Parmenides and Politicus also end with summaries.

[37] The conclusion to the Theaetetus shows a similar resemblance in manner to the early dialogues. After an enumeration of the refuted definitions of knowledge (210a) Socrates returns to the figure of the midwife. But his half-humorous moralizings upon his art and its effect upon Theaetetus are cut short by the recollection of an engagement at the porch of the King Archon. The last word is the promise of a meeting on the morrow (210d).

[38] See above p. 4, n. 4 for the use of the Socratic profession of ignorance to provoke a discussion. In the minor dialogues of search a repetition of this protest, and exhortation to continue the inquiry usually appear in the conclusion. Cp. Laches 200e–201a, Lysis 222e–223b, Char. 175b–176a, Rep. 354b.

[39] Cp. p. 58, n. 32. This same formula in Euthyph. 15e checks Socrates who is launched enthusiastically upon a fresh start in the argument (15cd) and closes the discussion. Socrates' reproachful reference to his purpose in beginning the inquiry is of no avail.

[40] Similarly in the Lysis at the close of the discussion a brief transitional paragraph (222e) summarizes their futile attempts to discover the friend. There follows a short dramatic scene (223ab), the humorous description of the noisy invasion of the half-drunken attendants, which puts a stop to Socrates' intended further investigations.

tion of temperance is full of characteristic humor and ironical self-depreciation. A playful reference (175e) to the charm of the Thracian physician recalls the beginning of the discussion. Socrates' exhortations to Charmides to persist in his self-examination and discover whether he has need of the charm are cleverly turned by the youth (176b), "And I think, Socrates, that I have great need of the charm, and for my part there is no reason why I shouldn't be charmed by you every day." The dialogue ends with Critias and Charmides vigorously protesting their unshaken confidence in Socrates.

The dramatic elements in the conclusion of the Laches are even more prominent. The decision in 199e that they have failed to discover what courage is leads naturally to a bit of amusing by-play between the two generals. Laches cannot resist gloating over Nicias' failure. Nicias retorts with a sharp rebuke and affirms his intention to continue the inquiry. Laches is still sceptical and advises Lysimachus and Melesias to consult Socrates rather than Nicias or himself with regard to the education of the boys. In this way a return is made (200c) to the topic with which the dialogue began. Lysimachus urges Socrates to consent to advise them, but Socrates makes use of his accustomed[41] profession of ignorance (200e-201a) to enforce the characteristic moral:—since they are all equally at a loss they must all seek out a teacher and learn. A meeting is appointed for the next morning.

From the final reluctant admission that completes the refutation of Protagoras (360e) the transition to the concluding summary is made easily and naturally by Socrates' earnest protest against the charge of contentiousness. He follows this up by a statement of their original positions with regard to the issue debated, and the strange reversal brought about by the argument. Finally by a literary reference to Prometheus and Epimetheus (361d), picking up the language of the myth told by Protagoras early in the dialogue, he leads up to the suggestion that they continue their investigations. But Protagoras, after a courteous expression of praise for Socrates' zeal and conduct of the argument, postpones further discussion εἰς αὖθις (361e) and both withdraw.

The Symposium is largely narrative and descriptive; its transitions are therefore of the type natural to such discourse. The closing

[41] See above p. 4, n. 4.

scene is introduced by one of the common[42] devices of narrative transition—reference to the speaker who has just finished (222c). The scene throughout is pure narrative flowing smoothly. Transitional particles[43] such as οὖν, μὲν οὖν, δή, μὲν–δέ, γάρ and καί link sentence to sentence in a natural sequence.

In the Phaedrus 278b a perfect imperative of completion and dismissal[44] πεπαίσθω is used in the transition from the discussion to the closing scene. The summary of the results of the inquiry is introduced under the guise of a message to Lysias. Socrates' rather patronizing encomium on Isocrates the Fair is called forth by the question of Phaedrus, who is perhaps loath to have his friend Lysias the only one criticized:—"What message will you send to him, Socrates, and how shall we describe him?" (278e) Unsatisfied in his desire Phaedrus then makes the suggestion, "Let us depart." The famous prayer of Socrates to Pan and the other gods of the place closes the dialogue (279b).

The closing scenes of the Gorgias and Republic[45] are structurally alike in this respect: in both Plato supplements the conclusions of dialectic by the religious confirmation of a myth of the underworld. In the Gorgias, the myth introduced by ἄκουε δή (522e) follows naturally upon Socrates' eloquent protest that "death no man fears, who is not altogether senseless and cowardly, but he does fear wrongdoing." At the end of the myth, 527a, a resumptive δ'οὖν introduces the final summary by Socrates of the important ethical conclusions of the dialogue and an exhortation to his companions to trust his argument rather than the thesis of Callicles.

The myth in the Phaedo is not, strictly speaking, a part of the conclusion, but immediately precedes the dramatic concluding scene of the dialogue. In purpose and relation to the argument, however, it corresponds exactly to the myths in the Gorgias and Republic. In its beginning (107c) the Phaedo myth is so much a continuation of the argument that it is not formally distinguished as a myth. But in 110b, the major portion of it is so introduced. In the transitional paragraph that links the myth to the dramatic conclusion of the dialogue Socrates carefully distinguishes myth from dogma and then,

[42] See p. 69.
[43] See p. 70.
[44] See p. 57.
[45] For the discussion of the conclusion of the Republic see pp. 44 ff.

in language that recalls the original theme of their discourse, explains the purpose of the myth: it is a charm to induce the conviction that death has no terrors for the philosopher, "And words like these he ought to croon over to himself as a charm, and that is why I lengthen out the tale." (114d). The exhortations to Simmias and Cebes and reference to his own approaching death-hour form a natural final step in the transition to the wonderful closing scene of the dialogue.

Strictly speaking the main divisions of a dialogue are the three fundamental elements, the dramatic introduction, the body of the discourse and the conclusion. However, the main discussion usually falls naturally into a number of important and well-defined parts. The transitions between these larger sub-divisions of the subject may very properly be considered as main transitions. In the minor dialogues of search important divisions in the argument are frequently marked by a change in the respondent.[46] The two parts in the main discussion in the Laches are so indicated. Laches' attempts at definition are confined to bringing out the temperamental aspect of courage (190e–193e). With the change to Nicias as respondent the intellectual aspect is introduced[47] and the argument becomes more subtle. In the paragraph of transition between the two parts of the

---

[46] See above p. 6, n. 11. The care with which Plato suits the character of the respondent to the tone of the discourse makes the change in respondents a very natural and effective means of transition.

[47] Similar advance from a simple to a more complex treatment is found in the Lysis and Charmides. In the latter Socrates' conversation with the youth Charmides (159a–162a) deals with the comparatively simple external aspects of temperance, while in the extremely subtle following discussion (162e–175a) Socrates interrogates the older, more experienced Critias. The transition scene (162a–e) is very amusing. By slily humorous disparaging comments Socrates cleverly goads Critias into taking up the defence of the definition of temperance as "doing one's own work," a definition for which he is evidently responsible in spite of his denial (161c).

The first part of the Lysis (207c–210d) is occupied with an edifying protreptic discourse in which Socrates and Lysis are the interlocutors. At its close (210e) Socrates recalls his purpose—to give the foolish Hippothales a lesson in addressing his friend. This first conversation is thus closely bound to the dramatic introduction. At the suggestion of Lysis Menexenus now becomes the respondent (211a). Socrates' playful protest and comment on the eristic disposition of Menexenus (211bc) account for the subtlety of the following discussion. In 213d Lysis again enters the argument, but the shift in respondents is only one element in this complicated transition. See below p. 72.

discussion the literary conceit of the personified argument[48] which bids them endure in the inquiry is followed by Laches' description of the effect of the elenchus upon himself. Then with the figures[49] of the huntsmen and the storm Socrates introduces the suggestion of summoning Nicias to their assistance. Socrates' harping upon ἀπορία and its derivatives adds a slight unifying touch.

The main discussion in the Gorgias falls naturally into three parts, conversations of Socrates with Gorgias, Polus and Callicles respectively. The transitions are simple and natural, the influence of the shift of respondents upon the character of the discussion unusually plain. Through Gorgias' unwillingness to deny that the rhetorician would teach justice to a pupil who needed that instruction he is finally involved in a contradiction and refuted by Socrates (461a). Polus intervenes and defends his master. After ironical commendation of Polus and injunctions to him to give up lengthy harangues[50] Socrates offers him his choice of questioning or answering. The discussion continues in 462b with Socrates as respondent, though he still guides the course of the argument.[51] The transition in 481b is similar. In spite of his scorn at Gorgias' scruples Polus himself is not entirely devoid of moral sense. He admits that to do wrong is more disgraceful than to suffer wrong, and this admission leads to his refutation.

[48] See below, p. 79.
[49] See below, p. 78.
[50] A further example of Socratic hostility to lengthy speaking is seen in Prot. 335. In the preceding debate whether the virtues are one or many Protagoras seeing himself refuted delivers a long speech (334a–c) on the relativity of the notion of good. With an ironical plea of forgetfulness Socrates protests his inability to continue the discussion unless Protagoras will cut his answers short, which the sophist refuses to do. This disagreement between the disputants, which results in a deadlock in the argument, serves as the transition to a dramatic interlude in which the other personages of the dialogue, anxious for the continuation of the discussion, urge various schemes of compromise and reconciliation.
[51] Compare Prot. 338de where for the sake of enabling the argument to proceed Socrates suggests that Protagoras assume the rôle of questioner for a time and later submit again to interrogation. Through this suggestion and its reluctant acceptance by Protagoras transition is made to one of the main divisions of the dialogue (339a–347a)—Socrates' interpretation of a poem of Simonides in which he cleverly parodies current methods of literary criticism. Again in 347b Alcibiades checks Hippias who is eager to make a display speech, with a reminder of the agreement (338d) that Protagoras should in turn submit again to the elenchus. This reference is an important link in the series of transitions which leads to the final discussion.

Callicles now interrupts with the amazed query whether Socrates is really in earnest or joking. Chaerephon replies, "He seems to me, Callicles, to be terribly in earnest, but there's nothing like asking him." With the utterly unscrupulous and cynical Callicles as respondent the character of the discussion changes. Socrates redoubles his irony and becomes uncompromising in his severity.

The analysis just given follows the external artistic frame-work of the dialogue. In the consideration of the main transitions of the Gorgias another important question arises, how is the connection made between the two parts of its double theme? Rhetoric is the ostensible topic of discussion; in reality ethics occupies as prominent, a place. The transition from rhetoric to ethics is managed very skilfully. In 455d Socrates leads Gorgias on to make immoral claims for rhetoric. Under the influence of ironical praise from him the unsuspecting sophist displays an immoral complacency at the idea of the rhetorician's power over the expert craftsman (456a, b). After these admissions Socrates is able by the introduction of the familiar[52] analogy of the arts and virtue to pass easily to the question of the attitude of rhetoric toward justice and injustice (459d), thus giving an ethical turn to the subject.

The Phaedrus is another dialogue with a double theme, in this case rhetoric and love. The first part of the dialogue, including the speech of Lysias,[53] 230e–234d, in praise of the non-lover, the rivaling speech of Socrates, 237b–241d, and the myth, 243e–257b, which is Socrates' palinode or recantation,[54] is occupied with love. By the literary criticism of the speech of Lysias, already suggested (234e, 235a, 236a) in the dramatic interlude connecting his speech with that of Socrates and taken up again in 258d, transition is made to the topic of rhetoric and the two parts of the dialogue are connected.

Like the Gorgias, the Meno is divisible into three parts and contains conversations of Socrates with three different persons. The main transitions, however, are not marked by the change in respondents. The first part of the dialogue (70a–80b), the attempt to define virtue, ends with Meno's complete puzzlement. He vividly describes the effect of the Socratic elenchus upon himself by the image

---

[52] Meno 90b; Laches 194e; 195b, 198d,e; Rep. 332c et al.
[53] See below, pp. 99 and 101.
[54] See below pp. 70 f.

of the torpedo-fish. After some bantering comment, the usual protest of ignorance from Socrates and the consequent suggestion that they conduct the inquiry together,[55] Meno introduces the sophistic quibble (80d) of the impossibility of inquiring into what one does not know. This passage serves as the transition to the second division of the dialogue. Instead of answering Meno's query directly Socrates has recourse to a myth[56] (81a) setting forth the doctrine that all learning is recollection. The myth answers Meno's objection and Socrates accordingly returns (81e) to his previous offer of joining Meno in an investigation of the nature of virtue. But Meno demands proof of the theory of recollection and this demand forms the transition to the dialogue with Meno's slave by which Socrates establishes the doctrine (82b–85b). These two subjects, the theory of recollection and its proof, occupy the second main division of the dialogue. Socrates follows up the conversation with the slave boy by some remarks on its significance, closing with an emphatic reaffirmation of his belief in the value of inquiry (86b). This rejection of the sophistic dictum that all investigation is fruitless serves as a natural transition to further discussion, and Socrates again (86c) suggests their joint inquiry into the nature of virtue. But Meno prefers to return to the original question of debate, whether virtue can be taught. The discussion with Anytus as to the existence of teachers of virtue occupies the central part of this third division of the dialogue.

In the following pages a more detailed outline of three of the longer and more complex dialogues is presented. An analysis of the Phaedo supports the comment of Archer-Hind that "every important issue turns upon some pertinent remark of Cebes."[57] The discussion begins (61c) with Socrates' qualification of his thesis that any philosopher worthy the name will be willing to die by the statement that he will not perhaps effect his own death, "for men say that is not lawful." At the end of Socrates' explanation of the theory that suicide is wrong Cebes raises the question (62c–e) how then the philosopher can desire to die and leave such good masters as the gods. The transition to the first general exposition of the reasons why the philosopher will welcome death is made by the figure of the defence (63b). Simmias suggests that Cebes meant to make his objection personal. How can

[55] See above, p. 8, and note 21.
[56] See p. 93.
[57] Archer-Hind, *Phaedo*, London (MacMillan), 1883, p. 41.

Socrates bear so easily to leave his friends and those good rulers, the gods? Socrates feels bound to explain his attitude toward death. He must make his defence as in a court-room. He will try to speak more convincingly to them than he did to the dicasts.

This figure of the defence recurs again.[58] It is picked up by Simmias after Socrates' first earnest statement of his faith that in the other world he will find gods wise and good. Again after the brief dramatic interlude of 63d-e it introduces renewed discussion. Socrates now states his thesis in even more vivid paradoxical form (64a), the true philosopher spends all his life practising death. Having defined death as the separation of the soul from the body, he brings forward several points[59] in support of his thesis. After considerable elaboration and expansion of these arguments, Socrates concludes in 69d-e with a recurrence to the figure of the defence.

At this juncture Cebes brings forward the objection that Socrates is assuming the immortality of the soul, a point that needs proof. The transition (69e-70a) is of the dismissive-introductive type,[60] combining a simple narrative formula[61] for marking a change in speakers with the common dismissive-introductive form with μèν and δέ, which marks a change in subject. Cebes desires proof (1) that the soul exists when the man dies, and (2) that it has power and intelligence. With the suggestion "Let us consider the question somewhat in this way" (70c), Socrates introduces an argument based on the old tradition that the souls of the dead exist in Hades and are born again on earth in new forms. Following the development and confirmation of this theory Cebes again (72e) interrupts to suggest[62] that the doctrine of recollection also implies the previous existence of the soul. In 77b Simmias calls attention to the fact that while the theory of recollection seems to establish the certainty of the preexistence of the soul and its intelligence in that former state, this proof fails to settle the question raised by Cebes (70a) whether the soul exists after death. As Cebes remarks (77c) the soul's immortality has only been

[58] Cf. p. 81, n. 37.
[59] These points are introduced by regular minor conventional phrases of transition,—σκέψαι δή . . . ἐὰν ἄρα καὶ σοὶ συνδοκῇ ἅπερ ἐμοί. (64c) τί δὲ δή (65a) τί δὲ δὴ τὰ τοιάδε 65d. See below pp. 53 ff., 68.
[60] See below pp. 56 ff.
[61] P. 69 below.
[62] καὶ μήν marks this suggestion as a transition to a new point. See below, p. 69.

half proved. Even after the assurance of Socrates that the combination of the two arguments given establishes also the soul's existence after death, Simmias and Cebes still hesitate (77e). Their dissatisfaction, vividly described by Cebes' picture of the child within us that fears death as some goblin, serves as the transition[63] to the discussion of indissolubility in general and the conclusions to be drawn from the soul's evident affinity to the indissoluble. With this argument from probablity the first main division of the Phaedo ends (84b).

The second section of the dialogue contains the objections of Simmias and Cebes to the preceding conclusions. Transition is made through a brief dramatic interlude (84c-85d) describing the effect of the previous discourse on the company. Simmias and Cebes are not satisfied, but hesitate to disturb Socrates with further questions. But Socrates by a pathetic comparison of himself to the swan who sings before his death persuades them that they ought to talk and ask him whatever they wish as long as the 'Eleven' allow. The objection of Simmias (85e-86d) is based on the Pythagorean theory that the soul may be a harmony dependent for its existence upon the framework of the body. The objection of Cebes continues his former protest (77c) that the existence of the soul after death has not yet been fully proved. The previous arguments have established the superior strength of the soul. It may probably exist after the body and may survive many bodies, but that it is altogether immortal and indestructible has not yet been proved. Cebes illustrates his position by the figure of the weaver who wears out many cloaks, but is outlived by the last which he weaves. Here another dramatic scene is interposed (88c-91c). By the vivid description of the despair of the company and the courageous protest of Socrates against misology Plato marks the importance of this crisis in the discussion. The Phaedo is a good illustration of one of Plato's favorite[64] methods of developing a theme. A partial or superficial view of the subject is first presented, only to be superseded or supplemented by further discussion.[65] His methods of transition to the more complete presen-

[63] The final step in the transition is found in the dismissive formula 78a b in which Socrates returns to the argument ὅθεν δὲ ἀπελίπομεν.

[64] The Republic, Phaedrus, Symposium and Theaetetus are other notable examples of this method. See Jowett-Campbell, *Republic*, Vol. II, p. 10.

[65] Hirzel, *Der Dialog*, Vol. I, p. 230—commenting on the development of the argument in the Phaedo—compares it to "a row of circles which touch one another, but yet each of them is complete in itself."

tation are varied. Sometimes, as at the end of Bk. I of the Republic, it is Socrates who is dissatisfied with his own conclusions. Here the suggestion of difficulties by the disciples provokes further discussion. In 91c-d Socrates continues the argument with a resumptive summary of the objections of Simmias and Cebes, which he proceeds to answer in turn. That of Simmias is less important and easily disposed of (91e-94e). The transition to the objection of Cebes is affected by the jesting personification of the argument (95a), incorporated in a dismissive-introductive formula. Theban Harmonia has been propitiated. We must now deal with Cadmus. In 95b-e Socrates again recapitulates the objection of Cebes which is fundamental and involves no slight matter (95e), the complete investigation of the cause of generation and destruction. There follows what may be an account of Plato's own philosophical experience[66] in the search for a final cause; at any rate it culminates in an exposition of the theory of Ideas as a working hypothesis. The importance of this conclusion for the argument is marked by a very brief dramatic interlude (102a) in which Echecrates expresses his approval of the acceptance of the theory. Resuming his narrative of the discussion Phaedo dismisses the question of the acceptance of the Ideas and proceeds (102b) with a continuative formula τὸ δὴ μετὰ ταῦτα to discuss their bearing upon the problem of change. The following final proof of the immortality of the soul depends upon a subtly fallacious application of the principle that opposite ideas are mutually exclusive.

In the Theaetetus "much of the argument is purely dramatic, directed only against the cruder forms of the theory combated."[67] A study of the main transitions in the dialogue is of value in the distinction between serious argument and mere eristic and persiflage. In his first attempt at defining knowledge, 146c, Theaetetus falls into the error of confusing definition with enumeration. As in the Meno (72a-c) Socrates corrects him, illustrating his meaning by a sample definition (147a). Theaetetus shows his comprehension of the method indicated by volunteering a definition of some mathematical terms. But he modestly protests his inability to define knowledge. His description of his previous efforts and failure leads Socrates to introduce the figure of the mid-wife (148e). This metaphor, which

[66] Burnet (*Phaedo*, Oxford, 1911, Introd. p. 38 ff. and note on p. 95) believes this to be a description of Socrates' intellectual experience.

[67] Shorey, *Unity of Plato's Thought*, p. 67.

plays an important part in the structure of the dialogue,[68] is developed through several pages. The return (151d) from this digression is made by a resumptive phrase[69] and reiteration of the demand for a definition of knowledge. The transition to discussion of Theaetetus' second definition, that knowledge is perception, is made by the common exhortation to joint investigation,[70] coupled with a reference to the metaphor of the midwife (151e). With this definition of knowledge as perception Socrates identifies the Protagorean dictum that man is the measure of all things. The result seems so paradoxical that he hazards the statement (152c) that Protagoras spoke in a riddle to the mob, while to his disciples in secret he told the truth. This playful remark, with its punning reference to the Ἀλήθεια of Protagoras, draws from Theaetetus the request for an explanation (152d) which serves as the transition to an interpretation of Protagoras with whose doctrine of relativity Socrates connects also the flowing philosophy of Heraclitus.[71] In 160d he reaches the conclusion that Theaetetus' definition of knowledge as perception is a very fine one, inasmuch as it agrees with these important teachings of Protagoras and Heraclitus. The image of the midwife now appears (160e) in combination with the further image of the ἀμφιδρόμια in transition to the criticism of Protagoras. A variation of the familiar[72] transitional formula of 'one little difficulty' forms the final step in the transition (161c). Socrates first overwhelms the doctrine with ridicule. In 162d Protagoras or some one of his defenders is represented as objecting to the methods used against him. The formula[73] ἄλλῃ δὴ σκεπτέον (163a) marks a fresh start in the argument. In the following pages 163-165 Socrates employs arguments which he himself admits to be eristic (164c-165a, b), justifiable in that they are directed against a crude, literal indentification of knowledge and perception. In 164e the literary conceit[74] of the personified argument is developed quite at length to introduce the defence of Protagoras. Socrates' promise to come to the aid of the orphaned argument (165a)

---

[68] See below, pp. 82 f.
[69] See below, p. 54, pp. 97–99; πάλιν δὴ οὖν ἐξ ἀρχῆς.
[70] See above, p. 8, n. 21.
[71] The half serious tone of 156-157 is significant.
[72] See p. 10, n. 27.
[73] See below, p. 54.
[74] See below, p. 79.

is picked up, after intervening persiflage, in 165e as the final step in transition to the defence. An interlude of by-play (168c-169c) results in establishing Theodorus as the respondent. In 169d the argument is resumed with a brief summary of the present position. It concludes in 171c with a περιτροπή[75]—the "truth" of Protagoras does not seem true to most people and must therefore be admitted by him to be false oftener than true. But here Socrates silences the protest of Theodorus by the assurance that he does not intend to rely upon this argument. The transition is made by a play on words.[76] By the distinction between sense impressions and the knowledge of what is healthful or advantageous Socrates passes to a more serious line of attack. At this point, however, the argument is interrupted (172b) by an eloquent digression, which Socrates himself recognizes as such (177b), in which he contrasts the life of the philosopher with that of the clever unscrupulous lawyer. The transition to this digression is very skilfully managed. By the mention of persons who are unwilling to accept the doctrine of extreme relativity when there is a question of the recognition of the advantageous in conduct, Socrates is led to speak of what such people consider wisdom. Here he pauses (172b), struck by the length of the digression into which he is being led. The protest of Theodorus that they have plenty of leisure picked up by Socrates (172d) makes a very clever and artistic transition[77] to the description of the life of philosophic leisure contrasted with the illiberal limited existence of the lawyer. In 177c Socrates dismisses the digression and returns to the previous argument. He now proceeds to serious criticism[78] of the doctrine of relativity and in 183b,c, the definition of knowledge as perception is defeated in so far as it "depends upon extreme Protagorean relativity or Heracliteanism, which makes all thought and speech impossible."[79] Theaetetus suggests (183d) that the definition should now be considered in relation to the theory of Parmenides and the philosophy of rest. Socrates, however, rightly rejects this suggestion, on the

[75] Note the invidious harping on ἀλήθεια.
[76] See p. 79, n. 32.
[77] See p. 97 f.
[78] See above p. 21. In the Theaetetus it is the protests of the defenders of Protagoras, cleverly introduced in various ways by Plato in 162d, 164e and 171c, that bring about the advance to really serious argument superseding the captious and eristic treatment of the earlier pages.
[79] Shorey, *Unity*, n. 523.

ground that it will involve them in too great difficulties. Through the figure of the midwife (184ab) he returns to Theaetetus as respondent and advances to a renewed discussion of his definition of knowledge from the point of view of physiological psychology. This interlude in which he plays with the order of the subject forms a very interesting variation in transition.[80] In 186d the conclusion is reached that truth is not in our sensations, but in the generalizations about them, so that knowledge is obviously something different from perception (186e). In 187a, b, as in 151d a resumptive formula and the demand for a new definition of knowledge mark a fresh start in the argument. Theaetetus suggests that knowledge may be true opinion. The question at once arises (188a), 'How can false opinion be explained?' Plato is careful to warn us by his leaving out of consideration learning and forgetting, that he is not serious in his apparent acceptance of the μὴ ὄν fallacy (189b). The following attempts to explain false opinion as "heterodoxy" (189bc) or to account for its existence by reference to the material images of the wax tablet (191c) and the aviary (197c) all prove futile. In 200 c,d, after a last reductio ad absurdum Socrates concludes that the attempt to discover the nature of false opinion is doomed to failure until they shall have determined the nature of knowledge. The transition here is enlivened by the conceit of the personified argument[81] which rebukes them for their desertion of her. A resumptive formula (200d) introduces the re-statement and further examination of the definition of knowledge as true opinion. It is easy to find a practical instance drawn from the experience of the law courts in which true opinion imparted by persuasion is not knowledge. The definition accordingly does not hold. In 201c,d, Theaetetus makes a third and final attempt and, recalling words that he has heard but forgotten till now, defines knowledge as right opinion with λόγος.[82] It is interesting to note the parallelism between Socrates' treatment of this and the earlier definition of knowledge as perception. In 152a-e he proceded to explanation and testing of the definition by connecting it with the doctrines of Protagoras and Heraclitus. So here (201d) in the interpretation of this definition he introduces a theory of elements and compounds for which he himself disclaims responsibility. As in the

[80] Cf. p. 94, n. 76.
[81] Cf. p. 79.
[82] See p. 92 for this literary device of the 'unexpected recollection.'

case of the earlier definition (cf 160d), the interpretation in terms of the theory seems at first entirely satisfactory (202cd). But as in 161c Socrates makes the transition to the criticism of Protagoras by expressing his wonder at one point, so now (202d) one of the statements they have just made fails to suit him. He believes that letters and syllables must be equally known. But perhaps the syllable is a whole different from the elements which compose it. The transitional phrase σκεπτέον καὶ οὐ προδοτέον, which introduces the discussion whether "whole" and "all" are the same, should be compared with the formula ἄλλῃ δὴ σκεπτέον in 163a which introduces a fresh start in the argument. "Whole" and "all" are proved to be the same (205a). The general conclusion follows (205b), that whether the syllable is made up of elements or is indivisible, syllable and elements are equally intelligible. This theory then like that of Protagorean relativity has proved an unstable basis for a definition of knowledge. In 206c he dismisses further consideration of the theory and turns to the discussion of three definitions of λόγος. None of these prove satisfactory; the definition of knowledge as right opinion with λόγος is therefore rejected (210a). An enumeration of the refuted definitions of knowledge introduces the brief dramatic conclusion.

That ancient scholars appreciated the structural difficulties of the Philebus is shown by the title of Galen's lost treatise, "Concerning the Transitions in the Philebus."[83] The following analysis of the logical framework of the dialogue does not claim to compensate for the loss of Galen's work; much less does it make any pretence to be an exhaustive outline of the philosophic content of the Philebus.[84]

The main divisions in the Philebus are not so clearly marked as in dialogues of less complexity. Frequent résumés of the argument[85] and restatements of the issue[86] attest Plato's realization of the difficulty of following the intricacies of the reasoning. Many slight passages of by-play[87] relieve the strain of argument and preserve

[83] Poste, *Philebus*, Oxford, 1860, p. 105, n. 4, for no apparent reason translates this 'On the abrupt transitions of the Philebus.'

[84] The unity of the Philebus has been questioned by Poste and others. Bury, in his edition (Cambridge University Press, 1897), maintains the logical coherence of the dialogue. In this he follows Trendelenburg, *De Platonis Philebi Consilio*, Berlin, 1837.

[85] 19c, d, 22b, c, 26b, 27b, 31a, 41b, 50b, c, 60a, b.

[86] 14b, 19c, d, 22c, d, 27c, 50e, 55c, 60a, 61a.

[87] 12b, 15c, 15e, 22c, 23b, 27e, 34d.

through the rather artificial framework the semblance of natural dialogue form. The dialogue begins abruptly without dramatic introduction. It is apparently the continuation by Socrates and Protarchus of a previous conversation of Socrates and Philebus. With the question (11b), "Shall we sum up the two views?" Socrates introduces an explicit statement of the question at issue, What is the good? Philebus contends that it is pleasure and enjoyment, Socrates that it is thought, memory, right opinion. In 11d Socrates makes the transition, by a similar formula of exhortation,[88] to a more precise re-statement of the problem, Which state or disposition of the soul is able to make life happy for all men? The phrase τί δ' (11e) introduces the possibility of a third claimant for first place. After this preliminary agreement as to the issue and the withdrawal of Philebus from the argument, the discussion is introduced (12b) by a transitional formula of exhortation.[88] Socrates begins with a playful adaptation of a familiar religious formula and reference to Philebus' identification of pleasure with Aphrodite. But in 12c he dismisses this little by-play and advances (with δέ) to the important point that pleasure is an equivocal term. He enumerates four unlike kinds of pleasure. Protarchus meets this point by the distinction that although these arise out of opposites they are not therefore themselves opposite. But Socrates rejects this distinction and demands a definition of pleasure as necessary for the argument (13b). Here Protarchus protests that pleasure qua pleasure is never bad. Socrates' criticism of Protarchus (13c-d) for thus blocking the argument and exposing them to ridicule as inexperienced in dialectic opens the way for the discussion of method which occupies the second sub-division of the dialogue. Before this is taken up, however, Socrates establishes the fact that knowledge also has many species and must be defined (13e-14b). This brief preliminary section of the dialogue closes with a re-statement of the issue (14b).

A transitional formula of exhortation (14c) introduces the general question of proper dialectic method. This is really, Socrates claims, only the old and troublesome problem of the one and many. Protarchus' failure to understand this statement[89] leads to explanation and illustration from Socrates. Finally in 16c he sets forth the method of

---

[88] See p. 54.
[89] See p. 88.

synthesis and diaeresis as the practical solution of their difficulties, whose use makes the difference between true dialectic and mere eristic. Demand for further explanation (17a) is followed as usual by elaboration and illustration. In 18d Socrates takes up the question, raised by Philebus (18a), of the bearing of this method upon the present discussion: it must be used in the enumeration and definition of the many species of pleasure and knowledge (19a). Protarchus delegates the task[90] to Socrates (19c), adjuring him to choose what method he will, so long as he solves their problem. With this recurrence to the issue and a warning that this is to be no mere resultless dialogue of search the section on method concludes (20a).

Before attempting the investigation of the species of pleasure and knowledge, Socrates returns (20b), by the literary device of the "unexpected recollection,"[91] to the suggestion already glanced at in 11d:—the good may be neither pleasure nor knowledge, but some third thing. He proposes, and Protarchus accepts, three criteria by which to test the good: it will be perfect, sufficient and desired above all things. An ordinary formula of exhortation (20e) introduces the application of these tests to pleasure and knowledge. Both fail and the true answer that the life to be preferred is a mixture of pleasure and wisdom is introduced (22a) as a suggestion by Socrates.[92] The question, "Do we understand?" prefaces a concluding summary (22b-c) which reverts in playful manner to the terms of 12b-c.

Transition to the modified form of the problem which now confronts them is made through the image of the second prize, introduced in a dismissive-introductive formula with μὲν οὖν and δὲ δή (22c).[93] Is pleasure or knowledge rather the cause of the excellence of the mixed life? Here the direct division of pleasure and knowledge into species is again postponed, by their inclusion in a larger classification of ὄντα. The first two classes, the ἄπειρον and the πέρας, are reached by a reference (23c) back to the discussion on method (16c). The third class is a *mixture* of these. Socrates introduces the fourth class, the *cause* of the union, by a playful jibe at his own stupidity (23d). The next step is the application of the method of synthesis and diaere-

---

[90] See below, p. 76, for description of the literary elements in the transition to this demand.
[91] See p. 92.
[92] See pp. 61 f.
[93] See pp. 56 f.

sis to these classes. The ἄπειρον is treated first (23e-24e). By antithesis transition is made (25a) to the πέρας, consideration of which had been postponed in 24a. The discussion of this class is brief, a mere enumeration of its main characteristics. A transitional εἶεν introduces the third class[94] (25b), in the treatment of which both ἄπειρον and πέρας are further discussed. A reference back to 23d introduces the fourth class (26e). The argument is led on by a series of suggestions from Socrates and ends with a brief recapitulation of the four classes (27b). A restatement of the question at issue (27c) serves as the transition to the next point for discussion:—the assignment to its proper class of each of the three lives under consideration. To facilitate discussion the mixed life of pleasure and knowledge is identified, without dispute, with the third class, the μικτόν. The satisfactory dismissal of this subject and advance to the consideration of pleasure is marked by a transitional εἶεν (27e). A change of interlocutors adds further emphasis. Pleasure, and pain too, since they admit of degree are easily assigned to the ἄπειρον. The question as to knowledge is now (28a) introduced with playful solemnity by Socrates. Philebus here gives way again to Protarchus, but he too declares himself at a loss. Socrates accordingly takes up the question himself (28c) and, with a glance at Philebus' charge that he is unduly exalting his god, knowledge, launches into an eloquent digression on the theme that mind is the king of heaven and earth. At its close (30e) Protarchus, though slightly bewildered, is content to admit that mind belongs to the fourth or causal class. Socrates frankly confesses his remarks to have been intended as a respite from their serious argument.

Transition to the next section of the dialogue is made through a formal résumé of the conclusions just reached about pleasure and knowledge (31a) and a statement by Socrates of the next point for investigation—the origin of pleasures and pains. A series of suggestions from Socrates leads to the conclusion that they arise in the mixed class[95] through dissolution and restoration of the harmony be-

[94] The following invocation to God is intended, Bury thinks (p. 42), to draw attention to the "combined difficulty and importance of what is to follow." Perhaps rather it is a fanciful way of leading up to the criticism (25d) that the πέρας has not yet been adequately treated—a somewhat captious criticism, for the enumeration of 25ab, though brief, is practically sufficient.

[95] The class *in* which they arise must not be confused with the class *to* which they belong.

tween the ἄπειρον and the πέρας. With the discussion of examples of this process the analysis of the species of pleasure has at last begun, as is recognized in 32b. In 32d the discussion is advanced by an announcement of plan; in the investigation of the second species of pleasure, the pure pleasures of the mind, it may be possible to discover whether the whole class of pleasure is always desirable. But before proceeding with this analysis, Socrates calls attention, with a formula of exhortation, to the neutral state which may, after all, be the most god-like. This subject, however, is postponed (33c) εἰς αὖθις, and by a recurrence to the image of the second prize, return is made to the discussion of the purely mental pleasures. This is found to involve some preliminary investigations, 1) of sensation and memory (33c-34c) and 2) of the nature and origin of desire (34d-35c). The renewed discussion of the states of pleasure and pain brings Socrates to a new question, (36c), should the terms true and false be used of pleasure? A warning of the importance of the subject and the necessity of being assured of its relevancy, ending with the familiar conclusion, "we must consider,"[96] forms the transition to actual discussion (36e). Considerable space is given to this problem for ethical reasons. Plato realizes the moral effect of the establishment of the applicability of the epithets true and false to pleasures. Socrates begins the argument with a more precise definition of the point at issue (37a) and a strong statement[97] of the view which he intends to oppose (37b). It soon appears that a discussion of true and false opinion is involved (37e). The ordinary transition-formulas of argument are varied here by the introduction of a reported imaginary conversation of a man with himself (38c, d), and the development of the comparison of the soul to a book (38e-39b). The existence of false opinion, and consequently of false pleasures and pains, and the similar illusory character of both are finally established (39c-40e). Socrates now proceeds, with τί δέ; to a further analogy between false opinions and false pleasures; in both falsity is synonymous with badness (40e). But Protarchus objects and Socrates accordingly postpones dealing with this point, until he has brought forward further proofs of the existence of false pleasures. The image of the wrestlers (41b) introduces the new attempt. A recapitulation of former ad-

[96] Cf. p. 54.
[97] Cf. Rep. 357-367 and Theaet. 166-168.

missions regarding the nature of desire (34b) and of pleasure (27e) leads to the conclusion that pleasures in themselves may be false and illusory, without reference to false opinion (42b). A transitional ἑξῆς ὀψόμεθα (42c) introduces yet another proof which Socrates seeks in a further consideration of the fact that pleasures and pains arise out of changes in the bodily state. In 42d he makes an abrupt and seemingly irrelevant reference to the interval when the body experiences no change, or rather when its motions are too slight to rise above the threshold of consciousness and produce either pleasure or pain. Through this renewed discussion[98] of the neutral life the doctrine that pleasure is mere freedom from pain is disproved (43c). Protarchus is convinced (43e) by the argument and illustrations of Socrates. The latter, however, seizes the opportunity to discuss the theory as upheld by certain philosophers. The transition is made (44a, b) by the common device of the interlocutor's failure to understand and the consequent need of explanation.[99] A statement of plan follows (44d-e). By this introduction of "the enemies of Philebus" the analysis of the nature and kinds of pleasure is continued with fresh interest. As the nature of anything is best seen from extreme cases, they now proceed (45e-46a) at the suggestion of Socrates to examine typical examples of the intensest pleasures which are really mixtures of pleasure and pain. This analysis of mixed pleasures ends (50b) with a general conclusion and summary. A paragraph of transition follows (50c-e) in which discussion of further instances of mixed pleasures is postponed. For the sake of the original question at issue the unmixed pleasures must next be analyzed. Socrates begins (51a) with a reference to the aforementioned (44b) physicists who deny the existence of true pleasures. His assertion of disagreement with them serves to introduce the following enumeration; while Protarchus' failure to understand leads at once to a fuller description of these pleasures (51b-52b). Now that the distinction between pure and impure pleasures has been adequately established (52c), Socrates proceeds to some further comparison of the two species; the pure pleasures belong to the class of measure, the πέρας, the impure or mixed pleasures to the ἄπειρον; the pure pleasures are true, the impure are false (52d-53b). Some further considerations as to

[98] Postponed in 33bc.
[99] See below, p. 88.

the nature of pleasure are now introduced to lead up to the formal rejection of the view that pleasure is the good. The transition is very abrupt. The conventional phrase τί δὲ τὸ τοιόνδε; (53c) forms the only preface to Socrates' question whether pleasure is not akin to generation rather than to essence. But as if to compensate for this lack of emphasis, in the immediately following discussion of the terms relative and absolute, the idea of the final cause is introduced (53e) in a playful over-elaborate style which draws instant attention to its importance in the argument. The conclusion (54c-d) is stated in the form of a syllogism: (1) pleasure is a generation coming into being for the sake of some essence and therefore not a final cause; (2) the final cause must be a good; (3) pleasure must belong to some category other than the good. This section of the dialogue closes with a further confirmation, a somewhat rhetorical argument, the absurdity of measuring moral qualities by the standard of pleasure (55a-b).[100]

The examination of the species of pleasure is now finished and by a sort of argumentum e contrario and figurative reminder of the issue Socrates passes to the examination of the species of knowledge. The analysis follows the method of dichotomy outlined in 16c, and is far less intricate than the discussion of pleasure. In 58a, in answer to Socrates' question whether dialectic is not the truest of the sciences, Protarchus introduces a slightly irrelevant point, the claims of Gorgias for rhetoric as the greatest of the arts. Socrates points out the irrelevancy (58bc) and proves the superior clearness and exactness of dialectic. In 59b he dismisses (with μὲν δή) all such personal disputes and returns (with δέ) to the point in question before the digression. The object of this highest science, dialectic, is true being. But the fairest things should have the fairest names. This contemplation of true being must therefore be called mind and wisdom, the very terms which Socrates has defended as rivals of pleasure (59d). With the completion of this analysis the main point at issue, the com-

[100] Poste, E. (*Philebus*, Oxford, 1860, p. 105, n. 4) argues that the *Philebus* is "a composition of two distinct fragments forming a well-proportioned whole, but rather carelessly soldered together in respect of some of the minuter touches." He considers the words πόλλη . . . ἀλογώτατα an interpolation added to effect this joining. But there seems to be nothing in this particular passage to support such a view; and the logical connection of the analysis of the species of knowledge with the theme of the dialogue is unmistakably clear.

parative claims of pleasure and knowledge, is really settled. Socrates' conclusion, triumphantly stated in 65a, is here implicitly established. The last pages[101] of the dialogue are a subtle blending of real argument with figurative and rhetorical elaboration.

The philosophic and structural unity of the Republic, attacked by Hermann, Krohn, Pfleiderer, Rohde, and other German scholars has been established beyond a doubt by the arguments of Hirmer, Zeller, and Campbell.[102] A detailed study of the main transitions of the dialogue only adds a further confirmation of their results. According to Hirmer's and Campbell's analyses the Republic readily falls into five main divisions, marked with careful transitions. The controversy begins over Book I, the introduction. Regarded by itself it seems a complete well rounded whole.[103] Hermann declares it to be an independent minor dialogue.[104] But though Book I may conceivably have been published earlier than the rest of the Republic[105]

[101] For a detailed analysis of these pages see below pp. 95 f.

[102] Hirmer, J., *Entstehung u. Komposition d. plat. Pol.*, Leipzig, 1897, J. P. Vol. 23. Zeller, *Phil. d. Griech.* 2, 1, 558 ff. Campbell, *Republic*, Vol. II, pp. 1-66; see also Shorey, *Unity of Plato's Thought*, pp. 78-82.

[103] Pohlenz, *Aus Platos Werdezeit*, Berlin, 1913, p. 209, n. 1, accepts the verdict of Sprachstatistik for the earlier composition of Book I, but argues that it could never have been independent. He bases his conclusion on the extent and tone of the introduction scene and on "die ganze Richtung nach der die Gerechtigkeit erörtert wird." Von Arnim, *Platos Jugenddialoge u. d. Entstehungzeit des Phaidros*, Leipzig, Teubner, 1914, p. 71 f., contests this view.

[104] See Hermann, *Geschichte u. System d. plat. Phil.*, Heidelberg, 1839, p. 537. Nusser, *Phil.*, vol. 53, 1894, p. 27, regards Book I as inorganically joined to the rest and is inclined to doubt its authenticity. Cp. Hirmer, p. 606 f., for a detailed refutation of these views. He enumerates the passages in Book I which contain anticipatory hints of the later discussion. See also Campbell, *op. cit.*, pp. 2-5.

[105] Von Arnim, *op. cit.*, pp. 71-109, bases his conviction of the earlier and independent publication of Book I in part on the result of his statistical stylistic investigations which establish its affinity with the Laches and Lysis. But granted that the method of Sprachstatistik does prove earlier composition we may still adhere to the view that even at that date Plato had in mind the plan of the whole Republic. Von Arnim finds further confirmation of his opinion in the fact that the development of ideas in Book I seems to place it earlier than the Gorgias and Lysis and later than the Laches and Protagoras. But as he seems fully aware (Vorwort, pp. III-VII) of the difficulties that beset such a line of reasoning and of the fallacies to be avoided (See Shorey, *Unity*, pp. 4, 19, and note 109) he would no doubt himself admit that at most it could establish only a strong probability. See Shorey's review of Von Arnim's book, *Class. Phil.*, Vol. 10, p. 334 f.

its complete suitability as an introduction to the whole work makes such a presumption unnecessary.[106] The chief feature of the brief descriptive narrative of the setting is the charming portrait of the aged Cephalus, artistically significant in that he is himself the perfect embodiment of that justice which is to be the theme of discourse. In the preliminary conversation of Socrates and Cephalus (328c-331b) the external connection between points seems slight; but throughout the passage one feels below the surface an inner connecting link, a unifying force, the aim of Socrates and Plato to guide the discussion into an edifying channel.[107] This determination finally culminates in 331c where Socrates abruptly generalizes the words of Cephalus into a definition of justice, which he proceeds to test by negative instances. In this way the subject of justice is introduced for consideration. In the course of the following discussion[108] the ethical problem as to the nature of justice and its rewards which is the real theme of the Republic is clearly indicated.[109] The most important subdivisions in Book I are marked by a change of interlocutors. In his conversation with Cephalus and Polemarchus Socrates is opposing popular opinions. After the interruption of the bullying Thrasymachus (336b) he turns to an attack on sophistic views of justice. The purely dialectical treatment of Bk. I sets the subject forth dramatically. But although by a train of subtle, sophistical reasoning Socrates succeeds in establishing against the sophist Thrasymachus his thesis that the just life is the happiest and that the life of injustice is altogether wretched, he concludes (354b, c) as in the minor dialogues with an avowal of "Socratic ignorance." The figure of the "feast of reason" used sarcastically by Thrasymachus

[106] In the beginning of Book II (357a) Plato refers to Book I as a proemium. Pohlenz, *op. cit.*, p. 209, note 1, thinks that while Plato designed Book I as an introduction he must himself have felt the lack of harmony between it and the following books. He regards it as possible that the Clitophon is an unfinished attempt to replace Book I with a more satisfactory introduction.

[107] Note the characteristic moral turn in 330d.

[108] See especially 344a, c, e; 347d, e; 352d.

[109] Hirmer *op. cit.* (p. 602) says that justice is only the nominal theme of the dialogue, that the state is the actual theme. Rather is it true that to the Greek mind the ethical ideal of justice is inevitably connected with political theory. Or one may say that the Republic like the Phaedrus and Gorgias has a double theme.

earlier in the discourse (352b) is introduced again in a dismissive formula[110] at the close of his refutation by Socrates (354a) and is picked up by the latter (354b) in transition to a concluding expression of dissatisfaction with the result of the argument. By this dissatisfaction of Socrates and his criticism of his own method of procedure in passing on to questions about justice before defining its nature, transition is made to the second main division of the Republic which comprises Books II, III and IV. The first few sentences in Bk. II continue the transition with Glaucon's protest against the inadequacy of the previous discussion and his appeal to Socrates to attempt a more scientific investigation (358b). The question is now resumed with the strongest possible statement of the case for injustice, put in the mouth not of Thrasymachus,[111] but of Glaucon and Adeimantus, who do not themselves believe it (358b-367e).[112] The brothers demand of Socrates (367e) proof of the value of justice per se. Thus the discussion is lifted to a much higher plane than that of Bk. I, and the fuller investigation that follows is amply justified. By the founding of the ideal state and the elaboration of the analogy between the state and the individual[113] the insufficient dialectical treatment of Bk. I is supplemented[114] by sociological and psychological arguments.

[110] "Let this then . . . be your entertainment at the feast of Bendis." ἑστιάσθω the perfect imperative of completion and dismissal is used. The phrase ἐν τοῖς βενδιδίοις recalls the dramatic setting, and thus has a unifying effect.

[111] The change of interlocutors at the beginning of Bk. II cannot fairly be used as an argument for its independence of Bk. I. The logical and artistic reasons for the change are sufficient to explain it. Glaucon and Adeimantus, who are in sympathy with Socrates, are the natural and fitting respondents in the serious exposition that follows. There is similar artistic motivation in the change of interlocutors within Bk. I and in the minor dialogues of search. See above p. 6, n. 11.

[112] Windelband (*Gesch. d. ant. Philos.* p. 225) maintains that Bk. I and Bk. II to 367e form an independent whole. He cuts off Socrates' answer in 368b making it thus a resultless dialogue on justice. Afterwards he revised his position, regarding 357-367 as a later inserted appendix to Bk. I. Cf. Hirmer, *op. cit.* pp. 595-6, 609-10 for discussion and refutation of Windelband's views. The higher tone of 357-367 separates it naturally from Bk. I; nor does its character seem that of an appendix, but rather transitional and introductory. Dreinhöfer (*Platos Schrift uber d. Staat*, p. 1-5) also groups the first ten pages of Bk. II with Bk. I.

[113] See below p. 82, n. 39.

[114] See above p. 21.

The transition to the founding of the state, the first important subdivision of this section of the Republic, is made by an image, the analogy of the large and small letters. The state is larger than the individual: therefore the nature of justice may be more easily discovered in the state (368e). The first sketch (369b-372a) describes the simple nature-state, whose growth is controlled by the principles of specialization and the division of labor. In such a city justice would appear, so Adeimantus suggests (372a), in the dealings of the citizens with one another. But Plato is aware that this simplest type of city-state affords no scope for the development of his political and ethical theories; accordingly he passes on (372e) to the description of a more luxurious city. The transition is made by a half-serious, half-comic interlude (372a-d), in which Glaucon protests against the swinish character of the life of the simple city. The problems of life in the more complicated city demand the addition of a new class of citizens, the warriors or guardians (373e). Discussion of the nature, education and method of selection of these guardians occupies the remainder of Bk. II and the greater part of Bk. III. The transition to the first of these topics is very skilful. In the long e contrario sentence (374c-d) which establishes the necessity of a warrior class, the development and illustration of the argument based on the division of labor introduces the ideas of μελέτη and ἐπιστήμη; φύσις, the third member of the triad is at once suggested to the mind.[115] A dismissive-introductive formula, with μὲν δή balanced by δὲ δή,[116] marks the advance from the subject of the guardians' natural endowment to that of their education[117] (376c). Socrates describes the kind of literature to be avoided (376d-378e) and lays down the principles which are to guide writers of tales in their city (378e-383c). The attack on Homer and the poets here begun is further developed in Bk. III which continues the description of the purified education. The transition is made by a sentence summarizing and dismissing, with μὲν δή, the closing subject of Bk. II and introducing, with the phrase τί δὲ δή; the next topic.

After discussing in detail both subject-matter and style of the literature and music suitable for the training of the guardians, Socrates passes to the subject of gymnastic. Again the transition is of

---

[115] These are the three necessary prerequisites for a perfect ἀγωνιστής.
[116] Cf. pp. 56 f.
[117] Notice also that the emphatic position of θρέψονται aids in the transition.

the dismissive-introductive type (403c). In 412b, waiving further discussion of details, he dismisses, with μὲν δή, this exposition of the main outlines of the education of the guardians,[118] and advances, with the transitional phrase τὸ δὴ μετὰ τοῦτο, to the question which of these warriors or guardians shall be our rulers. The following description (412c-414b) of the principles and tests which shall govern their selection is very brief.[119] The subject of the establishment of these regulations is now introduced (414b-c) rather abruptly by reference back to a previous (389b-c) discussion of the necessary lie. The allegory of the earth-born children, whose substance God mingled with different metals, gives a fanciful, semi-religious guarantee for the permanence of the ideal city (414c-415d). The book closes with a description of the manner of life which is to be required of the rulers to secure their disinterested patriotism (416d-417b).

The opening pages of Bk. IV (419a-427c) are occupied with a semi-digression or interlude in which various objections are answered. The connection with Bk. III is made through the first objection, that the guardians (or rulers) will not be happy. The points brought forward by Adeimantus and Socrates in support of this accusation repeat, with derogatory tone, the details of the eloquent summary at the end of Bk. III. With 427c[120] begins the transition to the second important sub-division of the argument in Bks. I-IV, the establishment of justice in the state and, by analogy, in the soul of the individual. Here also as in 368e, figurative language[121] inaugurates the transition, which is further marked by the summoning of Polemarchus and the others to a share in the conversation and by a restatement of the main points at issue. The ideal state has now been

---

[118] The passing reference in 412a to the need of an everabiding ἐπιστάτης or presiding genius, if the state is to be preserved, should be noted as an important anticipatory hint of Bks. V-VII, the higher education and the rule of the philosopher-king. (Cf. 497c.)

[119] Hirmer (pp. 610-11) notes that this chapter on the rulers is strikingly short and superficial, merely an appendix to the fuller treatment of the nature and education of the guardians. This incompleteness he considers a conclusive disproof of the independent existence of Bks. I-IV.

[120] Schleiermacher (*Platons Werke* III Th., I Bd., Berlin, 1828, p. 20) makes this the end of the second main division of the Republic. This seems wholly illogical. The program outlined in 369a has not yet been completed, as Glaucon reminds Socrates in 427d. Compare also Hirmer's statements, p. 587, note 1.

[121] See p. 79.

founded. By the assumption[122] that rightly organized means ethically good, Socrates introduces the subject of the four cardinal virtues (427e). Instead, however, of proceeding at once to the discussion of justice,[123] he first defines the other three virtues, wisdom, courage and temperance and determines in what part of the state each will be found. Finally in 434c he comes to the definition of justice in the state as the performance by each class of its own work. The next task is the discovery of justice in the individual, and to this Socrates makes transition (434d) by reference back to the analogy of the large and small letters (368d), recalling their object in founding the state. Developing the analogy between state and individual he assumes the existence of three principles in the soul (435e), appetite, spirit and reason, which correspond to the three classes in the state, the traders, auxiliaries or warrior class and the guardians or rulers. By a regular dismissive-introductive transition (τοῦτο μὲν δή . . . τόδε δὲ ἤδη) Socrates now (436a) passes from the recognition of these three types in the soul to the difficult question whether they are really three or rather one principle acting in three ways. By applying the law of contradiction, he proves the soul to be tripartite and establishes the opposition of appetite and reason (439e) and the relation of spirit as an ally of reason (440b). The virtues in the individual are now defined, and the definition of justice in the state is found verified in the individual (442d). As a further confirmation this conception of justice stands the test when judged by the criteria of popular ideas[124] of justice (442e-443c).

At the end of Bk. IV a provisional[125] conclusion is reached. Our dream is realized (443b). We have discovered justice (444a). After

---

[122] While this assumption in a sense begs the question, it does not interfere at all with the validity of the following arguments.

[123] See p. 94.

[124] See p. 84. This recurrence to the popular notions of justice, the subject of Socrates' conversation with Cephalus and Polemarchus in the early part of Bk. I, is not only an illustration of a common Platonic trait of style, but a confirmation of the unity of the Republic as well.

[125] Hirmer (p. 618) points out that the words ἀλλ' ὅμως (445b) continuing the discussion show that the conclusion reached in 444a–445b is regarded only as provisional. Compare also τύπον τινά in 443b. Similarly ὡς ἐν τύπῳ 414a, and οἱ μὲν δὴ τύποι 412b imply the incompleteness of the treatment of education. However, disregarding these plain hints does not affect the certainty that this conclusion is not final. The seeming completeness and independence of single

the acceptance of the analogy of health and disease (445a), the question of the comparative advantage of the just and the unjust life becomes foolish. Socrates now suggests that they complete the picture by an investigation of the forms of degeneracy in state and individual. The familiar[126] exhortation not to grow weary in the argument enlivened by the figurative expressions, "since we have reached this height" and "as from a watch-tower" marks the transition (445b, c). The opening lines of Book V are also transitional—a brief summary of the final conclusions of Bk. IV and Socrates' reiteration of his intention to discuss the types of degeneracy. At this point, however, the argument is interrupted by a long digression, Bks. V, VI and VII, in which the brief and inadequate treatment of the rulers[127] in Bk. II, 412b-414b, and the sketch[128] of their education given in 376c-412b are supplemented by the complete picture of the philospher-king and the detailed account of the higher-education and the Idea of Good. Very properly too is the paradoxical theory of the "community of wives," which needs careful explanation, postponed to this section of the dialogue.[129] These books, then, are the logically necessary complement of Bks. I-IV.[130] Transition to this third main division of the Republic is made very naturally and effectively by a dramatic interlude (449b-451b) in the style of Phaedo 84c. Polemarchus and Adeimantus, after whispered consultation, demand an explanation of the proverbial phrase κοινὰ τὰ φίλων as applied by Socrates in

---

sections of an argument has been already noted (see above, p. 21) as a common peculiarity of Platonic composition. Many times the discussion will seem at an end only to be renewed again. In Bk. I, for example, the argument might have concluded at 336a, 343a or 347e.

[126] Compare also Theaet. 151d, 157d; Protag. 333b; Crat. 411a, 428a; Soph. 261b, 264b; Rep. 435d.

[127] See above p. 37, n. 119.

[128] Plato indicates clearly that this is only a general outline. Cf. 412b and 414a as well as the reference to "the longer way," that is the higher education, in 435d which is picked up in 503a, 504b.

For a general discussion of this subject see Jowett-Campbell, *Plato's Republic*, Vol. II, pp. 8-12.

[129] Compare 502d, where Socrates refers to his earlier omission of these topics as "a piece of cleverness which was not of much service."

[130] For a full discussion of the technical and artistic reasons which determined the contents of Bks. V-VII and a convincing refutation of the theories of Krohn, Christ, Pfleiderer and Rohde that they are superfluous or a later addition to Bks. I-IV, see Hirmer, pp. 612-620.

423e-424a to women and children. The scene is enlivened by figurative and proverbial expressions and by a playful use of legal terminology. Socrates prefaces his explanation by characteristic[131] protests of ignorance and unwillingness.[132] The unforced naturalness of this transition scene is a strong argument against the "separatists."[133] Throughout this section of the dialogue the transitions are managed with great skill. Especially noteworthy are the recurrent comparison of the wave and the chimerical wish (εὐχή), external means by which Plato secures a unity of tone for the whole.[134]

The first part of Bk. V (451c-471c) is occupied with the discussion of the two paradoxes concerning women, Socrates' explanation of his application of the phrase κοινὰ τὰ φίλων. The first paradox, the community in education between the male and female guardians is shown to be both possible (451c-456c) and desirable (456c-457b). By the figure of the waves of ridicule transition is made to the consideration of the second paradox, the community in wives and children for the guardians. The question of its possibility is postponed by Socrates[135] (458ab), until he shall have established its desirability. But when this has been accomplished, 466c, a digression on war affords a further excuse for postponement. The transition to this digression is entirely natural, and the German critics[136] who find here an awkward juncture of two independent sections seem quite unjustified. Socrates has mentioned in a casual way in his concluding summary (466c) that the women also will go to war. It is quite in accord with Plato's manner that such a point should be singled out for further development.[137] Glaucon's recall of Socrates from the digression is equally natural. He reminds him that meanwhile the possibility of the second paradox still remains unproved. His

[131] See p. 4, n. 4.
[132] Plato seems to have forgotten the original scene (328a).
[133] Notice too that the interlocutors do not make their request immediately after the provisional conclusion of 445b. Socrates first sets forth his program for the discussion of injustice. Bks. I-IV are thus also closely bound to Bks. VIII and IX.
[134] For a full treatment of these, see pp. 72 and 84.
[135] See p. 84.
[136] For a discussion of the question see Hirmer, p. 619. As to the subject-matter of this digression, Hirmer shows that no more suitable place in the Republic could be found for this section.
[137] Compare Laws 692d-693c, 655a, b; Phaed. 258e-259e; Phil. 28c-30e.

brief reference to the results of the previous discussion includes mention of the content of the digression, which is thus adequately connected with the rest of the argument.

This conversation between Glaucon and Socrates (471c-473c) forms the introduction to the second main division of this section of the Republic (471c-502c). The possibility of the community of wives appears (471e) dependent on the possibility of the existence of a state such as they have been describing. To the latter question Socrates accordingly turns his attention. A brief discussion of the relation between the ideal and actual prefaces the statement in 473d of the third and greatest paradox, the government of the state by philosopher-kings.[138] The explanation and establishment of this paradox involves thorough investigation of the nature of the true philosopher and proof of his fitness for rule.[139] Finally in 501e Socrates and Adeimantus agree that enough has been said to satisfy their opponents and in 502c Socrates declares that the possibility of the existence of their state has been proved.

With a dismissive-introductive transition Socrates now passes to the question of the education by which these philosophic guardians will be produced—a subject which occupies the remainder of this section of the dialogue. Plato's symbolical expression for the complete education of the guardians is the knowledge of the Idea of Good (505a). He leads up to the discussion of this by a brief but adequate résumé (502e-503e) of the main points in his earlier insufficient treatment of the rulers in Bk. II, 412b-414b, and by reference (504a) to the tripartite division of the soul and the definitions of the four virtues established in Bk. IV. The discussion of the Idea of Good is concluded by the development and interpretation of the image of the divided line (509d-511e) and the following allegory of the cave (514a-519c), an allegory of "the ascent of the soul into the intellectual world" (517b). The application (519c-521c) of this allegory of education to the guardians of the ideal state introduces in a natural way the discussion of the details of their higher education, the means

---

[138] For description of the further development here in transition of the figure of the wave, see p. 72.

[139] Windelband (*Gesch. d. ant. Philos.*, p. 225) concludes his second main division of the dialogue with 486. This view seems unjustified by anything in the subject-matter or its arrangement. Hirmer (p. 620) believes his error due to a misconception of the allegory of the ship of state (488 f).

by which they shall attain to that necessary knowledge of the Idea of Good. Of the two criteria (521d) by which Socrates proposes to test his scheme of education the first is the only one of real importance, viz. that the subject studied should train the mind to think in abstract terms. The second test, that it should be useful for a soldier is only a detail in the literary frame-work of the dialogue: it is inserted merely because the guardians are drawn from the warrior class. Applying these two criteria, gymnastic, music and the arts are rejected (521e-522b) and mathematics, applied mathematics and dialectic are selected as materials for the higher training of the guardians (522c-540c).

At the close of Bk. VII the discussion of the ideal state and its philosophic rulers is declared complete (540d-541b). The fourth main division of the dialogue comprises Bks. VIII and IX. Bk. VIII opens with a transitional εἶεν expressing satisfaction with the preceding and introducing a brief summary (543a) of the contents of Books V, VI and VII. Following, in 543b καὶ μὴν introduces a reference to still earlier conclusions—the provisions of the last pages of Bk. III. These summarizing statements lead naturally to the return from the digression which is effected (543c-544b) by a recapitulation of the program outlined by Socrates at the end of Bk. IV and by reference back to the scene at the beginning of Bk. V. The image of the wrestler (544b) serves as the immediate transition to the resumption of the argument from the conclusion of Bk. IV.[140] Socrates now enumerates (544c) the four degenerate types of state and individual which are to be the subject of their discussion, viz. the timocratic, oligarchical, democratic and tyrannical. He reminds his hearers that this investigation is necessary to complete their inquiry as to the comparative happiness of the life of justice and injustice (544d-545a). By a reference back to the analogy of the large and small letters (368d) he introduces a brief outline of the method of procedure which he proposes to adopt (545b). Finally, in 545c, with a transitional phrase of exhortation,[141] he turns to the first topic of discussion, the development of timocracy from the ideal state. But here the general problem arises, why should there be any degeneracy? Plato recognizes that dogmatism is out of place here. Accordingly he dismisses

---

[140] See above p. 39, n. 126.
[141] See p. 54.

the subject with the myth of the so-called Platonic number (546a-547a). Transition to the myth is made by the playful adaptation of a Homeric quotation[142] (545d, e) and in 547a the incorporation in a similar manner of a few words from Homer[143] into the final summarizing sentence of the myth and the playful reference to the language of 545d, e mark the return to the discussion of the rise of timocracy. The sketch of the origin and character of the timocratic state now follows (547b-548c). With a dismissive transition waiving further details Socrates next passes to the description of the character and origin of the timocratic soul. In 550c this is declared complete and he turns to the consideration of the rise of oligarchy. The formula of transition here is varied by an adapted quotation from Aeschylus.[144] After the description of the oligarchical state he takes up the nature and origin of the corresponding individual (553a-555b). Democracy is next to be considered (555b), and the democratic nature (558c-562a). Lastly, there are left for discussion tyranny (562a-569c) and the tyrannical soul (571a-576b). Throughout this description of the four degenerate types of state and individual the transitions are simple and unelaborate, mostly of the ordinary dismissive-introductive type which is especially suitable for the connection of sub-divisions in the argument, where any decided break in the continuity is undesirable.[145]

Transition to the next main division of this section of the dialogue is marked by a change of interlocutors and by Socrates' recurrence (576b) to the ethical problem, which is the main issue of the Republic, and of which he reminded his hearers in 571a, before beginning the description of the tyrannical man. With the completed picture before us of the worst and wickedest type of soul, the tyrannical, we are ready for the comparison with the best and most just and the judgment as to their happiness. The provisional conclusion of Bk. IV is here substantiated by three formal arguments. The first proof (576c-580c) for the superior happiness of the just man is based on the parallelism between state and individual and is, in a way, a summary of the whole social and political thought of the Republic. The

[142] Il. XVI 112.
[143] Il. VI 221; XX 241.
[144] Aeschylus, Septem 451 and 570.
[145] For an account of the recurrent metaphor of the drones as a unifying element in Bks. VIII and IX, see pp. 81 f.

formal proclamation of the five types of state in order of their happiness and the other references to the methods of theatrical contests merely serve to emphasize the importance of the conclusion. With a transitional εἶεν δή and a regularly balanced[146] dismissive-introductive formula advance is now (580c-d) made to the second proof.[147] This argument is psychological, based on the tripartite division of the soul:—the man who seeks ideal pleasures will have experienced also, in a fair degree, the lower pleasures, while the man devoted to honor or gain has no knowledge of the higher pleasures. The third and crowning[148] argument, the metaphysical, rests on the proof of the unreality and impurity of all pleasures except those of the wise man (583b-588a). In 588b Socrates dismisses (with εἶεν δή) as satisfactory the conclusions of the discussion up to this point. By again recurring to the main theme of the dialogue he now introduces, as supplemental confirmation of the three formal arguments, two figures, the image of the beast in man (588b-591c) and the analogy of health and disease in the soul (591c-592).

With the end of Bk. IX the ethical demonstration of the superior happiness of the just life is complete. Bk. X is an appendix in which Plato adds to his elaborate sociological and psychological arguments the religious confimation of a myth describing the rewards of the just man in the other world. The eloquent moral climax of Bk. IX is thus superseded by a higher spiritual climax.

The transition to this concluding book is especially interesting. The myth does not follow immediately upon the conclusion of Bk. IX. Plato was aware that sustained grandeur becomes wearisome. Accordingly Bk. X opens with an abrupt return (introduced by καὶ μήν) to the question of the banishment of poetry from the ideal state. This interpolated[149] discussion closes with a summary (607b-

[146] See pp. 56 f.
[147] Pfleiderer (*Platonische Frage*, p. 74) and Rohde (*Psyche*, p. 558) maintain that 580c-588a is a later insertion. This arbitrary act is due solely, as Hirmer believes (p. 622), to their desire to exclude all mention of the Ideas from Bks. VIII-IX and so in their opinion establish their priority to Bks. V-VII. No illogicality of thought or awkwardness in connection at this point, which might support their position, can be pointed out.
[148] The literary features of the transition to this argument are described in Chap. III, p. 75.
[149] Aside from the artistic reasons for the introduction of this discussion at this point, we should also note that its position is logically appropriate. Plato

608b) emphasizing the importance of the question for the moral welfare of the State and leading naturally to Socrates' suggestion (608c)[150] that the greatest rewards of virtue have as yet been undescribed. The following proof of the immortality of the soul, which is introduced by Socrates' picking up of the word 'great,' is needed here to pave the way for the myth. In 612a Socrates dismisses further discussion of the soul and returns to the question of the rewards of justice. The speech of the two brothers at the beginning of Bk. II is taken up and the prizes received by the just man at the hands of gods and men briefly enumerated. Finally, in 613e-614a Socrates passes by a dismissive-introductive transition to the myth which details the rewards of justice in the life to come. In Bk. I we have the picture of the aged Cephalus, the just man, whose eyes are already turned in hope to the other world (330d-331b); now at the close of our long investigation the tale of the experience of Er the son of Armenius strikes the same key-note and rounds the dialogue into one harmonious whole. The single impressive summarizing sentence which follows the myth and concludes the dialogue sustains the note of eloquence. In its climactic conclusion the Republic is unique among the dialogues, most of which end on a quiet commonplace note with their highest point of feeling before the conclusion.[151]

There is one important transitional problem in connection with the Republic which has been only partially disposed of by the above analysis of the main transitions of the dialogue, and that is the division into books. Are the transitions from book to book real and do the divisions so made mark important logical divisions in the argument? The transitions between Books I and II, IV and V, VII and VIII and IX and X coincide with the main transitions of the dialogue.[152] The separation of the three larger portions of the dialogue into parts corresponding in length as nearly as possible with the

---

is here supplementing his earlier polemic of Bk. III by psychological and philosophic arguments based on the intervening sections of the dialogue. For a full justification of this view see Hirmer, pp. 624-625 and Shorey, *Unity of Plato's Thought*, p. 81.

[150] Hirmer (p. 588) calls attention to the fact that this second sub-division of Bk. X, like the first, begins with καὶ μήν.

[151] Compare the Gorgias, Philebus, Cratylus.

[152] Hirmer (p. 589) thinks the division into books originated in the recognition of these main divisions.

introduction and conclusion is both natural and artistically desirable, provided always that it does not violate the logical structure by emphasizing minor sections at the expense of the more important. In the Republic there is no suggestion of any attempt at a slavish equalization of the number of pages in the several books, though they are fairly uniform in length.[153] The transitions from book to book are sometimes slight, but they always mark definite and logical subdivisions of the subject. The transitions between Bks. II and III and III and IV have been described already.[154] Books V and VI are very closely connected. In the last part of Bk. V Socrates distinguishes the nature of the true philosopher from that of the "lover of opinion." Bk. VI 484a dismisses with $\mu\grave{\epsilon}\nu\ \delta\acute{\eta}$ further consideration of this question and passes on to discuss the comparative qualifications of the two types for leadership (484b). Bk. VI ends (511d, e) with a brief dismissive summary of the interpretation of the image of the divided line. Bk. VII begins rather abruptly, with a mere phrase of transition $\mu\epsilon\tau\grave{\alpha}\ \tau\alpha\hat{\upsilon}\tau\alpha\ \delta\acute{\eta}$ introducing the allegory of the cave. The slight transition is perfectly adequate because of the general parallelism between the two images, a parallelism pointed out by Socrates himself (517b).

The description of the tyrant state and its rise out of a degenerate democracy is declared complete at the end of Bk. VIII (569c). Bk. IX begins (571a) with the simple statement of the tyrannical type of individual as the next topic for discussion. Objection may be made that the book-division here is arbitrary, that the description of the tyrannical soul should logically be included in Bk. VIII. On the contrary there is both logical and artistic justification for its position at the beginning of Bk. IX. The first formal argument for the superior happiness of the just man hinges on the contrast which his life presents with that of the tyrant. The description of the tyrant then, stands in a closer logical and artistic relation to the content of Bk. IX than to that of Bk. VIII, and is rightly included in Bk. IX. The fact that Socrates refers to the ethical problem in 571 before he begins the account of the tyrannical soul is a clear hint of this relation.

[153] Birt (*Das antike Buchwesen*, Berlin, 1882, p. 442) gives the following statistics as to the distribution of lines:—Bks. I 1279, II 1147, III 1393, IV 1147. V 1371, VI 1165, VII 1128, VIII 1128, IX 941, X 1147.

[154] See pp. 36 f.

From the above analysis it is evident that the division of the dialogue into books is neither arbitrary nor inartistic. It does not fall within the scope of the present paper to attempt to settle the much disputed question[155] whether Plato himself is responsible for this division or whether it is the work of a later hand. In so far as the decision depends on evidence from the study of the transitions there seems to be nothing to prevent the acceptance of the division as Platonic. However, there are other considerations which give us pause. In order to reach a final conclusion it would be necessary to examine the evidence for an earlier and less satisfactory division[156] into six books, as well as to investigate fully the claims based on the analogy of proved instances in the case of Homer, Hesiod, Thucydides, Xenophon and Aristotle.[157]

Turning directly from the structurally perfect Republic one is impressed by the comparative irregularity of the Laws. But if this "masterpiece of Plato's old age" falls short of perfect symmetry in outline, it is at least logically coherent. Plato was perhaps himself aware that the discourse is a little rambling. At any rate, throughout the Laws, there is a very evident effort to guard against logical confusion by frequent cross-references,[158] repetitions,[159] résumés and anticipations[160] of the main plan. Several quasi-apologies[161] for the numerous delays and false starts and for the "many apparently trifling customs or usages" that "come pouring in and lengthening out our

[155] The division into books is regarded as unplatonic by Schleiermacher, p. 4 ff.; Hermann, *Pl. Ph.*, pp. 537, 693; Steinhart, *Einl.*, p. 66 ff.; Christ, *Pl. Stud.*, p. 22; Birt, *Das ant. Buchw.*, p. 447; Nusser, *Platons Politeia*, p. 95 ff.; Dreinhöfer, *Pl. Schr.uber d. St., 24* anm.; Hirmer, p. 589-91.
The following attempt to prove the division Platonic. Schneider, *Ausg.* I, p. xii f.; Rettig, *Prolegomena ad Platonis Rempublicam*, Bernae, 1845.

[156] Pohlenz (*Aus Platos Werdezeit*, Berlin, 1913, pp. 207-237) deals at length with the tradition of an earlier edition of the Republic, but does not touch the question of Bk. division.

[157] For a thorough discussion of these arguments see the literature of the subject noted above.

[158] 649b, 652b, 672c, 682e, 685b, 688a, 696c, 701d, 705b, d, 707d, 773e, 781e, 796e, 793b, e, 794b, 798d, et al.

[159] 659d, 688b, 699c, 733, 662-63, 740e, 743e, 754c, 770c, 774c, 812a, 822e, 876d, 887b.

[160] 682e-683a, 699e, 701cd, 702a, 722c-723e, 768c, d, 864c.

[161] 768c, d; 642a, 682e, 701cd, 723d, 799d, 780d.

laws,"[162] show that Plato fully recognized the possibility of criticism of the structure of the dialogue.

In brief the plot of the Laws is as follows. There is practically no dramatic introduction. The subject of discussion is introduced almost in the form of a title περί τε πολιτείας τὰ νῦν καὶ νόμων (625a). A very slight description of the setting and personages of the dialogue accompanies the announcement of the subject. But although without dramatic introduction, the Laws is by no means lacking in prefatory matter. The first four books and nearly half of the fifth (to 734d, e) comprise a lengthy prelude or preamble, sociological, historical, and ethico-religious, which seems many times on the point of coming to an end, but is repeatedly continued to include further introductory material. In 734e general preliminary considerations are at last dismissed. The transition is made through a formal dismissive-introductive statement of plan. "Let the preamble to the laws which has been here given suffice; after the preamble the law must needs follow; or rather, to speak more accurately, a sketch of the laws of the state." The laws of the constitution of the state are considered first; provisions for the distribution of land, the appointment of officials and the establishment of courts of appeal. These enactments are each in turn prefaced by appropriate explanatory and hortatory preambles. In 768c-e further discussion of the courts of law, the election of magistrates and other details of political administration is dismissed for the present. The Athenian declares that they are now ready to proceed to the actual laws of the state. After a rather lengthy proem, he at length begins with the enactments regulating marriage and the birth of children which occupy the remainder of Bk. VI. Bk. VII treats of education, Bk. VIII of festivals, games, military exercises and other institutions of civil life. Bk. IX is concerned with criminal offences. Bk. X is an eloquent ethico-religious preamble to all the laws of sacrilege. The transition to this from Bk. IX is made by the introduction at the beginning of Bk. X of a general law summing up all acts of violence. The recognition of the importance of offences against the Gods leads naturally to the following protest against atheism. Books XI and XII are occupied with a great variety of miscellaneous laws relating to dealings between man and man. With the discussion of the regulations regarding burial the

[162] 793d.

laws strictly speaking are completed—960b. It remains to make provision for the permanence of these institutions. The impressive description of the nocturnal council of guardians which shall be the eyes and mind of the state, acquainted with the final aim of the lawgiver[163] "a guard set according to law for the salvation of the state,"[164] forms the final main division of the dialogue. In the transition to this conclusion a familiar[165] literary transitional device, the respondent's failure to understand, is followed up by an analogy. We need some preserving power in our state which shall be like the third of the Fates, Atropos, the unchanging one. In this way the full explanation is naturally introduced.

That the Laws, while loose in structure is by no means devoid of plan the above brief analysis will show. The long rambling proemium presents the greatest structural difficulties; and it is this section of the dialogue that contains the largest number of those transitional summaries, reminders of the plot and similar devices by which Plato strives to correct the impression of disorder.[166] The discussion in Bk. I begins very abruptly with the Athenian's question[167] as to the aim of certain Cretan institutions, the common tables and the gymnastic drill. Cleinias replies that their purpose is to inspire courage in war. In the course of the following criticism, which is based on the fundamental principle that laws should be framed with a view to all the virtues rather than one alone, the Athenian describes at length the purpose and procedure of an ideal lawgiver. This description, 631b-632d, is an excellent summary of the entire plot of the dialogue and an argument for the belief that from the start Plato held the plan of the whole firmly in his mind. The discussion of courage, resumed after this summary, is followed (635e) by an investigation of institutions relating to temperance. In this way the subject of the disciplinary value of pleasure is introduced. The discussion of this sociological problem continues through Book II and is worked out with considerable detail:—the use of wine, the song and dance and festive intercourse in general are considered. The transition from Book I to II

[163] 964e–965a.
[164] 968a.
[165] See p. 88.
[166] See above pp. 47 f. notes 158–162.
[167] 625c.

is made by a simple progressive formula τὰ δὴ μετὰ τοῦτο ὡς ἔοικε σκεπτέον and the dismissal of the point last established.

Book II closes with a summary of the discourse on wine and music. The sociological part of the proemium is now complete. At the beginning of Bk. III instead of taking up gymnastic[168] Plato turns to the question of the origin of society. He attempts to disguise the lack of real connection between Books II and III by the use of the transitional formula ταῦτα μὲν οὖν δὴ ταύτῃ. Book III contains several important recapitulations and reminders of the plot. When in the course of the historical survey of the development of civilization the settlement of Lacedaemon is reached, it is made the excuse for a reference back to the beginning of the dialogue, and the recognition of the prefatory and preliminary character of all the preceding discussion of wine and music.[169] In 683e there is a further reminder of the same conclusion, that in pursuing the discussion of the settlement of Lacedaemon they are really resuming the original inquiry after a digression. 688b again strikes the keynote of Bk. I that the lawgiver should regard all virtue not merely a part. In the latter pages of Bk. III the balance of powers in the Spartan consitution is contrasted favorably with the extreme tyranny of Persia and the equally extreme democracy of Athens. Here the Athenian pauses to consider the best method of procedure and call attention to the importance of the previous arguments.[170] Megillus calls for a fuller explanation and thus transition is made to an emphatic statement of the characteristic Platonic doctrine that degeneracy in morals follows degeneracy in music. In 701c there is an important reminder of the plot and plain hint of Plato's purpose in inserting frequent summaries—"Now why have I said all this? Because it seems to me that the argument, like a horse, ought to be pulled up from time to time, not let to go with mouth unbridled as it were." The following résumé in 702a leads to the discovery that their conclusions may be put to practical proof in the new Cretan colony which is about to be sent out. This foundation of the Cretan state forms the external basis of the whole plot of the Laws. Its introduction here serves as the transition to Book IV which continues with further particulars as to site and the character of the colonists. 705de reiterates, in the tone

[168] The discussion of gymnastic is postponed until 813, 814.
[169] 682e–683a.
[170] 699e.

of Bk. I, the warning as to the final aim of the lawgiver. 715e marks the completion of the historical and political section of the proemium and the beginning of a general ethico-religious preamble which is introduced under the guise of an address to the new colonists (716-718). In 718b-d an idea is introduced which is of the utmost importance in the literary frame-work of the dialogue,[171] that of the need of a special preamble prefixed to each law, whose purpose shall be the predisposition of the citizens to obedience. This idea is developed with considerable repetition by the use of image and quotation and by the example of a specimen law of marriage with appropriate preamble.[172] Finally, in 722c d, the entire discussion up to this point is formally recognized as the general prelude or preamble to the laws which are to follow. After a little further explanation and generalization of the idea, the transition to Bk. V is made (723e-724a) by dismissive introductive formulas marking out the order of discussion. A part of the ethical principles necessary to their preamble have already been sufficiently developed in the hortatory address to the new citizens on the honors due to the gods and their parents.[173] It remains to complete this unconscious[174] proemium by a further prefatory ethical discourse dealing with all that relates to the souls and bodies and possessions of the citizens. The completion of this ethico-religious preamble occupies the first half of Bk. V. In 734e the general preamble comes to a sudden end. Its dismissal is marked by the use of the imperative of completion.[175] The next topic for consideration is the laws of the constitution. Further preliminary material, a special proemium to these laws, is here introduced, 734e, by the figure of weaving, which suggests the idea of purification. In 737c the laws are at last begun.

Throughout the main body of the dialogue the plan is fairly regular; laws with their preambles prefixed follow one another in the order given in the general outline above.[176] The literary significance of the idea of the proemium to the plot of the laws is here apparent. Most of the numerous passages of eloquent moral reflection, the philo-

[171] See below.
[172] 721.
[173] 716–718.
[174] 723d.
[175] καὶ τὸ μὲν προοίμιον τῶν νόμων ἐνταυθοῖ λεχθὲν τῶν λόγων τέλος ἐχέτω.
[176] See pp. 48 f.

sophical and political disquisitions, by which the dry detail of legislation is constantly varied, are introduced, either explicitly or implicitly as preambles to the following laws, not as irrelevant digressions disturbing the unity of the whole. It is interesting to note[177] that the formula of transition from preamble to law always suggests the hope that the persuasive power of the former will render the threats and penalties of the law unnecessary.

The transitions from book to book in the Laws are simple and abrupt. That from Bk. III to IV is the only one that shows any attempt at artistic elaboration. Bks. XI and XII are absolutely unconnected; a mere formula forms the only transition between Books II and III. In the case of the other books a single transitional sentence of the dismissive-introductive type at the beginning of the book, connects it with the preceding   But it is not only the book to book transitions in the Laws that are abrupt and stereotyped; the transitions throughout the dialogue are more artificial, less natural and artistic than in the Republic. Increased formality and precision are indeed characteristics of the style of all the "later" dialogues.[178] The abruptness and conventionality of the book to book transitions in the Laws is therefore no convincing argument that the division into books is unplatonic. As in the case of the Republic, however, the question is far too complicated to be decided by a mere consideration of the transitions.[179]

[177] See Shorey, "Plato's Laws and the Unity of Plato's Thought," *Class. Phil.* IX, p. 369.
[178] See Appendix, pp. 102 f.
[179] See above, p. 47.

CHAPTER II

Minor Conventional Forms of Transition

An exhaustive account of the transitional phrases, formulas and particles, of the more stereotyped methods of transition used by Plato would require a sentence to sentence analysis of the dialogues. No one has as yet attempted such a comprehensive summary,[1] though various statistical studies of particles[2] supply some material. The present paper aims merely to collect and illustrate some of the commonest of the conventional forms of transition which appear in the dialogues.

Most numerous of all is that type in which the transition is made by some explicit reference to the discussion. This may take the form of a command to investigate, an exhortation to joint activity, a statement of the need of inquiry, a brief prothetic declaration of intention, or a detailed description of the method and purpose of the subsequent discussion. Forms of σκέπτω, ἐπισκέπτω, σκοπέω, ὁράω, λέγω, ἐννοέω and similar verbs, deictic pronouns and adverbs[3] such as τοῦτο, τόδε, τοιοῦτον, οὕτως, ὧδε and αὖ, combined with inferential particles like οὖν or δή constitute the usual vocabulary of this variety of transition. Its simplest type is a brief formula of command,[4] intro-

---

[1] Hans v. Arnim's *Sprachliche Forschungen zur Chronologie der Platonischen Dialogen* (Wien, 1912) p. 9, contains a very slight attempt at classification of formal transitions. There are also several treatises on methods of transition used by the Greek orators. These have been listed by R. D. Elliott, *Transition in the Attic Orators*, Menasha, Wis., 1919, pp. 1–9.

[2] See Appendix, p. 102, n. 1.

[3] Deictic pronouns and adverbs are always transitional because they contain in themselves elements of repetition and incompleteness. See Mendell, *Latin Sentence Connection*, pp. 19, 33, 91-93, 142 f.

[4] Cf. Protag. 316c, 323a, 355a, 356c; Euthyph. 9d, 10a, 12d; Crat. 389a, 392c; Rep. 477c, 485b, 524d; Gorg. 476b, 495c; Theaet. 147a, 153d, 158e, 182a, 166d, e; Meno 71c, d, 73d, 82b, e, 90b, 93b; Phil. 49b, 29b, d, 31b, 32e, 39e, 45d; Phaedo 67e, 70d, 73b, 74a, 80a, 92c, 96d, 104b; Char. 161b; Phaedr. 243e, 263d, 264c, 268a; Laches 189c, d; Lysis 206b, 217c; Crito 51c, 50a; Symp. 199cd,

ducing a new subject for investigation. Thus in Gorg. 510b the words σκόπει δὴ καὶ τόδε mark the advance to the next point in the argument. The resumptive formula of command which introduces a fresh start in the discussion[5] should be included here. αὖθις and πάλιν ἐξ ἀρχῆς are its common catch-words. So Euthyphro 11b, ἀλλὰ πάλιν εἰπὲ ἐξ ἀρχῆς. For the formula of exhortation to joint inquiry[6] compare Protag. 330b—φέρε δή . . . . κοινῇ σκεψώμεθα ποῖόν τι αὐτῶν ἐστιν ἕκαστον. In Char. 167ab the formula which marks a fresh start in the argument takes the form of an exhortation.[7] πάλιν τοίνυν . . . . ὥσπερ ἐξ ἀρχῆς ἐπισκεψώμεθα. The transitional statement of the need of investigation as an obligation is also very common. The verbal in -τέος may be used[8] as in Theaet. 203e, σκεπτέον καὶ οὐ προδοτέον ‛οὕτως ἀνάνδρως μέγαν . . . λόγον; χρὴ or δεῖ may take the place of the verbal.[9] Thus Laches 184e, οὐκοῦν καὶ νῦν χρὴ πρῶτον αὐτὸ τοῦτο σκέψασθαι and Rep. 461e δεῖ δὴ τὸ μετὰ τοῦτο βεβαιώσασθαι παρὰ τοῦ λόγου. The simple formula, whether of command, exhortation or obligation, may be slightly elaborated by the injunction not to be discouraged;[10] so in Protag. 333b, ἴθι δή . . . . μὴ ἀποκάμωμεν ἀλλὰ καὶ τὰ λοιπὰ διασκεψώμεθα. Compare also Crat. 411a, οὐκ ἀποδειλιατέον ἀλλ' ἐπισκεπτέον.

The transition may be made by a prothetic statement of intention or purpose.[11] The myth in Protag. 320c is introduced by a clear indication of the speaker's feeling with regard to it, δοκεῖ τοίνυν μοι, ἔφη,

---

210e, 217b, 214b, 215b, 207c, 200a, d, 176a. For a further discussion of these formulas, see *infra*, p. 62.

[5] Cf. Theaet. 151d, 184b, 187a; Protag. 333d; Phaedo 105b; Meno 79e, 90c; Char. 160d; Laches 198a, 191e.

[6] Cf. Theaet. 151e, 157e, 203a; Laches 192e, 198c; Euthyph. 7a, 9e; Lysis 216c, 218d; Laws 649b; Soph. 261d, 267e; Gorg. 476a; Protag. 343c; Meno 78c, 86c, 87e, 88a; Phil. 11d, 12b, 14c, 34d, 35d, 37a, 39c, 51e, 54a; Rep. 372a, e, 334e, 436b, c, 473b, 489e, 576b. For the interrogative form with βούλει οὖν see *infra*, p. 60.

[7] Cf. pp. 74 f. and Laws 626e.

[8] Cf. Theaet. 164c, 179d, 181b, 204b; Euthyph. 15c; Phaedr. 244a, 246b; Meno 96d; Char. 158d; Phil. 26e, 28a, 34d, e, 36e, 46b, 49a.

[9] Cf. Laches 179b; Theaet. 192a; Meno 79c, 87c; Symp. 189d; Crat. 384c.

[10] Cf. Theaet. 151d, 157d; Rep. 445b; Soph. 261b, 264b; Phil. 21d; Crat. 428a.

[11] Cf. Protag. 324c, 338c, d, 353c; Phil. 18a, 26b; Symp. 177c, 186b, 189d, 194e, 204d; Gorg. 473a, 464b; Rep. 491a; Phaedo 96a; Crat. 404e; Pol. 267d.

MINOR FORMS OF TRANSITION

χαριέστερον εἶναι μῦθον ὑμῖν λέγειν. Again in Protag. 342a Socrates prefaces his interpretation of the poem of Simonides with an announcement of his own intention, ἐγὼ τοίνυν, ἦν δ' ἐγώ, ἃ γέ μοι δοκεῖ περὶ τοῦ ᾄσματος τούτου πειράσομαι ὑμῖν διεξελθεῖν.

Transitions in which the reference to the discussion is confined to a stereotyped formula illustrate the external method of connection, which may or may not be strengthened by further transitional elements. In many cases the idea of the formula is reinforced by or developed into a more definite description of the plan and method of the discussion.[12] These detailed outlines of method are characteristic of the later and more difficult dialogues. They are especially frequent in the Laws. So in Laws 632d-e the common transitional resumptive formula, ἐξ ἀρχῆς πάλιν ἔμοι γε δοκεῖ χρῆναι διεξελθεῖν καθάπερ ἠρξάμεθα is elaborated by a description of the proposed order of topics in the discussion.

A transitional discussion of method may include protest against or rejection of some unsatisfactory course of procedure.[13] So in Theaet. 191 a-c in a lengthy outline of his plan for further investigation Socrates condemns a previous decision.[14] The summarizing formula μὴ γὰρ οὕτω τιθῶμεν, ἀλλ' ὧδε serves as the final explicit link in transition to the reconsideration of the question, "what is false opinion." A criticism of former methods may be combined, in a transitional passage, with a resumptive recurrence to the main question at issue. The Meno affords several examples of this type of transition;[15] for instance in 77a, after Socrates has finished his series of sample definitions, he urges Meno to redeem his promise to define virtue κατὰ ὅλου and stop "making many out of one."

The transitional resumptive statement, summary, or reminder of the issue is not always associated with criticism. It is constantly used to mark the return from a digression;[16] it provides a method for

---

[12] Cf. Crito 48b-e; Gorg. 505e, 506a; Laches 189e, 197e; Meno 86d, e; Symp. 201d, e; Protag. 333c; Phil. 20c-e, 23b-e, 28c, d, 31b, 32c, d, 34c, d, 44c, d; Phaedr. 237c, d; Laws 626d, 638b, 643a, 799d et al.; Rep. 368e, 369a, 545b.

[13] The introduction of the idea of criticism or correction is a common transitional device. Cf. *infra* p. 63, also p. 93.

[14] Cf. Theaet. 162e-163e, 166d, e, 187d, e, 188c, d; Rep. 354; Symp. 180c, d; Laches 190c, 185b-c.

[15] Cf. Meno 74a, 93a-b.

[16] Cf. pp. 98 f.

advancing the argument common in all the dialogues,[17] especially suited to the more complicated and difficult.[18] A brief resumptive summarizing phrase often serves to introduce the conclusion of a passage of reasoning.[19] The phrase οὕτω δὴ τούτων ὑποκειμένων is so used in Protag. 359a.

Cross reference to a previous point is a usage closely allied to the resumptive transition, though far broader in its scope. Its effect is always unifying and in many cases it is also transitional. Advance to a new step in the argument is frequently made through the appeal to a previously established point. So in Laches 198a the reference back to a former fundamental assumption (190d) is an important element in the transition to renewed discussion. This use of cross references in the progress of the argument, in binding one division to another and making the whole logically coherent, is distinctly transitional. In many instances, however, their purpose is much more general; they contribute to the unity of tone, the artistic unity of the dialogue.[20] Of such a character is the reference to Thrasymachus and his views in Rep. 367a-c, and the recurrence to the style and philosophy of Thrasymachus in Adeimantus' objections in 419. Cross references naturally occur more frequently in the longer, more complex dialogues, but they are used in all the dialogues.[21]

A prothetic statement of the point next to be considered is often combined with the formal dismissal of a preceding discussion. This dismissive-introductive form of transition is very common.[22] It may be used to mark either a minor advance or an important division of the argument. The type admits of numerous variations, but the principle underlying them all is the characteristic Greek fondness for balance. The expression of dismissal is usually marked by the

---

[17] Cf. *supra*, p. 54, n. 5; also Euthyph. 9a; Protag. 349a-c.

[18] Cf. p. 26, notes 85 and 86; p. 47, notes 158, 159, 160; also Theaet. 169d; Phaedo 91c-d; Protag. 359ab; Gorg. 506c; Rep. 543ab.

[19] Cf. Meno 76d, 98a; Phil. 48c; Symp. 178c, 180b; Phaedo 66b, 80ab, 111a.

[20] Scholars have made extensive use of cross references in proving the structural unity of the Republic. Cf. pp. 33–45.

[21] The following list of cross references in the Laches and Phaedrus will illustrate the usage. Laches 186e ref. to 184d; 187c to 179b; 191c to 190e; 193d to 188d; 198a to 190d. Phaedrus 243e ref. to 237b; 249d to 245b; 249e to 249b; 250c to 250b; 253cd to 246a; 257a to 243b; 262d to 259b; 265a to 245bc; 265b to 244.

[22] For a literary variant of this type cf. pp. 89 f.

MINOR FORMS OF TRANSITION

particle μέν alone or strengthened by οὖν, δή or τοίνυν, while the new topic of discussion is introduced by a balancing δέ, δή or δὲ δή.[23] Both parts of the transition admit of all the variety of expression noted in the consideration of introductive formulas (pp. 53-55), i.e., command, exhortation, statement. In the dismissal the perfect imperative, which implies completion, is more frequently used than the present. Deictic pronouns and adverbs form an important transitional element in both dismissive and introductory statements. Protag. 332a illustrates the simplest method of balance, with μέν and δέ, the formula of exhortation, and the deictic pronouns, τοῦτο pointing backward and τόδε forward. τοῦτο μὲν ἐάσωμεν, τόδε δὲ ἄλλο ὧν ἔλεγες ἐπισκεψώμεθα.[24] For the use of the imperative in the dismissal[25] compare Laws 734e—καὶ τὸ μὲν προοίμιον τῶν νόμων ἐνταυθοῖ λεχθὲν τῶν λόγων τέλος ἐχέτω, μετὰ δὲ τὸ προοίμιον ἀναγκαῖόν που νόμον ἔπεσθαι. In Rep. 456c both the balancing particles are strengthened by an inferential δή. καὶ ὅτι μὲν δὴ δυνατά, διωμολόγηται; Ναί. ὅτι δὲ δὴ βέλτιστα, τὸ μετὰ τοῦτο δεῖ διομολογηθῆναι.[26] In Theaet. 182c one point is selected to continue the discussion; the others are dismissed with μὲν τοίνυν. τὰ μὲν τοίνυν ἄλλα χαίρειν ἐάσωμεν . . . . οὗ δ' ἕνεκα λέγομεν, τοῦτο μόνον φυλάττωμεν, ἐρωτῶντες.[27] Similarly, μὲν τοίνυν and the perfect imperative ὡρίσθω are used in Rep. 439e to dismiss the discussion of the two elements in the soul, desire and reason, while δὲ δή introduces the investigation of the third element, "spirit." Dismissals with μὲν οὖν are especially common, not only in Plato,[28]

---

[23] In a few cases the balance is differently marked. So in Rep. 444a an inferential δή is followed by γάρ. ἔστω δή . . . . μετὰ γὰρ τοῦτο σκεπτέον οἶμαι ἀδικίαν. Again in Rep. 607b ταῦτα δή . . . . ἀπολελογήσθω in the dismissal is balanced by an introductory προείπωμεν δέ. Compare Rep. 553a, 562a; Laws 820e.

[24] For other cases of the μέν–δέ balance, cf. Protag. 347b, 358a; Phaedr. 246a, 248a, 265c; Symp. 180c, 186a, 201d, 207b; Pol. 287a; Rep. 432b, 580c; Laws 745e; Euthyph. 3c; Phil. 12c, 15a, 28e; Meno 86b, 89d; Phaedo 69e, 95a.

[25] Cf. Laws 698a; Rep. 392c, 503b; Meno 92d; Phil. 28a; Phaedr. 246d.

[26] For other examples of μὲν δή in the dismissal, cf. Theaet. 173b, 187a; Gorg. 470b; Laws 672e, 698a, 832ab; Symp. 196a, 216c, 220c; Meno 93e; Phil. 59b; Phaedo 78ac; Phaedr. 238d, 246d; Rep. 392c, 376c, 386a, 415d, 436a.

[27] For other examples of μὲν τοίνυν in dismissal cf. Theaet. 150a; Rep. 427c, 502a; Symp. 200a; Phil. 32b; Rep. 611a, 613e; Phaedr. 264e; Soph. 245e; Laws 779d.

[28] For other examples cf. Protag. 321d, 319c, 323c, 324c, d, 355e; Theaet. 180c; Laws 816d, e; Symp. 178a, 183c, 195c, 196b, d, 204b, 221c; Phil. 13ab

but in other Greek writers as well.[29] In Laches 183d in transition to the climax of the amusing anecdote of the scythe-spearman μὲν οὖν is used to dismiss uninteresting details. τὰ μὲν οὖν ἄλλα οὐκ ἄξια λέγειν περὶ τ' ἀνδρός· τὸ δὲ σόφισμα τὸ τοῦ δρεπάνου τοῦ πρὸς τῇ λόγχῃ οἷον ἀπέβη. A formula of dismissal may be reinforced by a detailed dismissive summary.[30] So in Rep. 350d the formula τοῦτο μὲν ἡμῖν οὕτω κείσθω is preceded by a resumptive summary of conclusions, introduced by δὲ οὖν. Compare also Laws 689c-e where the dismissive formula τοῦτο μὲν τοίνυν οὕτω κείσθω is followed by a long explanatory summary. At the close of the paragraph the dismissal is repeated with another formula, ταῦτα μὲν οὖν, καθάπερ εἴπομεν ἄρτι, λελεγμένα τεθήτω ταύτῃ and the next topic is introduced by δὲ δή.

The Platonic dialogues contain also another type of dismissive transition, that in which discussion of a subject is either passed over altogether, or dismissed by a formula of indefinite postponement.[31] The subject so postponed is not usually treated again.[32] αὖθις or εἰς αὖθις is a common catch-word of the dismissal; the new topic for discussion is usually introduced immediately with δέ.[33] So in Protag. 347b Alcibiades checks Hippias from making a display speech and recalls the agreement between Socrates and Protagoras as to further

---

16e, 22c; Phaedr. 238d, 239b, c, d, 246a, 250c; Rep. 357a, 347de. The combination μὲν οὖν may be further strengthened by an intensifying δή. So in Rep. 359b, 360d; Phaedo 112e.

[29] Cf. Isoc. IV 43d, 47c, 61d; Thuc. I 123, 15, 40; III 64; Isaeus VII 11; Isoc. II 17d; V 93d, 98d, 100a, 101b; VII 151b; VIII 164b, 171c, e; Lysias X 31; XII 47; XIII 51; XIV 3; XXIII 13; XXIX 8.

[30] Cf. Rep. 398bc; 461d-462a; Phaedr. 245b; Laws 674a-676a; 697c-698a; 822cd; 832ab.

[31] Cf. p. 78 for a literary elaboration of this method of transition.

[32] This is the view defended by Adam (*Republic of Plato*, Vol. I, pp. 46–7, Cambridge, 1905) in a note to Rep. 347e. He cites Siebeck's unsuccessful attempt to prove that "phrases of this sort always refer either to some future dialogue contemplated by Plato, or to a later part of the same dialogue." (Siebeck, *Zur Chron. d. Pl. Dialoge*, pp. 121 ff.)

An occasional instance occurs in which a subject postponed receives further attention. Rep. 466a takes up the question of the happiness of the guardians dismissed in 420d. The phrase εἰς αὖθις is not used in 420d, but appears in 466a where Socrates recalls the previous dismissal. Compare Phil. 42c-43e, where the discussion of the neutral life dismissed with εἰς αὖθις in 33b is again renewed.

[33] Cf. Protag. 357b; Rep. 347e, 430c; Euthyph. 6c; Meno 99e; Tim. 50c; Symp. 194e; Euthyd. 275a. In Symp. 175e ὀλίγον ὕστερον is used instead of αὖθις. Cf. καὶ τάχα in Soph. 254b.

debate. εἰς αὖθις γε· νῦν δὲ δίκαιόν ἐστιν ἃ ὡμολογησάτην. This formula of postponement may be used to bring a dialogue to an end;[34] thus Euthyph. 15e, εἰς αὖθις τοίνυν, . . . νῦν γὰρ σπεύδω ποι, καί μοι ὥρα ἀπιέναι.

In Laches 181c a μὲν οὖν of dismissal is combined with a postponing αὖθις; δέ returns to the point at issue. ταῦτα μὲν οὖν καὶ σὺ ποιήσεις καὶ ἡμεῖς σε καὶ αὖθις ὑπομνήσομεν· περὶ δὲ ὧν ἠρξάμεθα τί φάτε.[35] Another paraleiptic formula[36] is used in Rep. 412b, in passing over minor details[37] of legislation. χορείας γὰρ τί ἄν τις διεξίοι τῶν τοιούτων; εἶεν and the phrase τὸ δὴ μετὰ τοῦτο introduce the next point. Phil. 50c-e furnishes an example of a more elaborate paraleiptic transition. In dismissing further discussion of the class of mixed pleasures Socrates acknowledges that much remains to be said. He has purposely treated the difficult case of comedy in order that Protarchus might excuse him from the rest. "I fancy," he continues, "that I may obtain my release without many words, if I promise that tomorrow I will give you an account of all these cases. At present I want to sail in another direction." Protarchus agrees to the postponement. Socrates then states as the next topic of discussion the unmixed pleasures. The particle τοίνυν and a dismissive prepositional phrase μετὰ τὰς μειχθείσας ἡδονὰς connect this statement with the preceding.

In the case of a subject to be treated again the postponement is usually to a time more definite than the vague εἰς αὖθις.[38] So in Phil. 18a Socrates postpones his answer to Philebus' question as to the relevancy of his discourse on method until he shall have given some further illustrations. He recurs to the question in 18d, dismissing his explanations as adequate.

[34] Cf. Protag. 361e; Crat. 440e.

[35] Cf. Phil. 41a. In Phaedr. 268a a regular dismissive formula of exhortation is used in a paraleiptic transition; in Rep. 400c a dismissive perfect imperative is similarly used.

[36] Cf. Phaedr. 241e; Euthyd. 291 b.

[37] The omission of detail may be implicit rather than explicit, as in Theaet. 179c. Compare the explicit paraleiptic statements in Phil. 26b; Gorg. 465b; Rep. 471e, 484a, 548d; Laws 772a. The use of ἀλλά, alone or in combination with γάρ, οὖν or δή, in waiving further discussion should be noted here. Cf. Meno 92c; Phaedr. 261c; Rep. 530c; Theaet. 177e; Phaedo 100a.

[38] Compare Phil. 24a with 25 b, d; Laws 768c, d with 853 f, 956 f.

Transition to further discussion may be made by an assumption evading proof or dismissing difficulties.[39] So in Euthyphro 9c-d, Socrates dismisses by an assumption the consideration of Euthyphro's treatment of his father and is thus enabled to resume the quest for the definition of piety. In Theaet. 185e, Socrates avoids by an assumption the necessity of proof. He declares that Theaetetus has done him a kindness in releasing him from a very long discussion, "if you are clear that the soul views some things by herself and others through the bodily organs." The division of things into two classes is a further transitional element in this passage.

Gorg. 454e illustrates the introduction of a dichotomy[40] as a method of advancing the argument. Transition to the amended definition of rhetoric is made by the division of persuasion into δύο εἴδη. Note the introductory interrogative formula βούλει οὖν . . . θῶμεν.

Akin to this method of formal dichotomy is the transition made by formulating a distinction and offering a choice.[41] Of this nature is the transition in Laws 654c to the discussion of what is the standard of the beautiful. So in Meno 73e Socrates' question whether justice is virtue or a virtue serves as a transition to the effort to show Meno the distinction between genus and species. The piece of inductive reasoning in Meno 77b-78b by which Socrates proves that all men desire the good furnishes a more extended illustration of this method of advancing the argument by formulating distinctions. Meno has just given his definition of virtue as ἐπιθυμοῦντα τῶν καλῶν δυνατὸν εἶναι πορίζεσθαι. With a view to using the most sharply contrasted terms Socrates asks permission to substitute the word ἀγαθῶν for καλῶν. Meno consents and Socrates states the question he wishes to discuss— Do some men desire evil and others good? Do not all desire the good? Meno will not agree to the latter, but declares explicitly that some men desire evil. Socrates then formulates a distinction and offers Meno his choice; do those who desire evils do so in ignorance, thinking them goods or are they aware that they are evils? Meno thinks that there are instances of both. Once again Socrates makes Meno

[39] Compare the adoption of a method of hypothesis in Phaedo 100a and Meno 86e.
[40] Cf. Theaet. 198d; Laws 629c; 646e; Crat. 424c; Phil. 18b c; Phaedr. 277b; Rep. 397b.
[41] Cf. Theaet. 196c, 203c; Meno 73d, 78d.

agree to the explicit statement; some men desire evil, knowing that it is evil. He now makes this question still more definite, do they desire that this evil should become their possession? Meno believes that desiring a thing can have no other meaning. Socrates proceeds with another dichotomy; do they desire this ignorantly, thinking that evil is a benefit, or do they know it to be an injury? Again Meno boldly asserts that there are instances of both. "Do you really think that they recognize evil as evil, when they think it is a benefit?" continues Socrates, and by this question forces from Meno the reluctant admission (with γε) that he does not think they do. With an inferential οὐκοῦν Socrates states his conclusion; these men do not really desire evil, but good, in their ignorance mistaking the one for the other. Meno grudgingly assents.

Socrates now returns, with τί δέ; to the other group, those who desire evil, knowing that it is injurious. Meno agrees that they must be aware that they will be injured by it. With an introductory ἀλλά, pointing the contrast of the new thought, Socrates asks whether these men do not think that those who are injured are wretched, in so far as they are injured. Meno agrees that this too must be so. With a view to strengthening the statement, Socrates picks up the word ἀθλίους with δέ and asks whether they do not consider the wretched as κακοδαίμονας, unfortunate. Meno assents, and, with an οὖν marking the inference, Socrates asks whether anyone wishes to be wretched and unfortunate. This seems to Meno impossible. Socrates now states his conclusion with ἄρα; no one chooses evil unless he wishes to be wretched and unfortunate, for wretchedness is just desiring evil and getting it. Meno's assent is an explicit statement of the conclusion toward which Socrates has been working, "You seem to me, Socrates, to speak the truth; and I think that no one chooses evil."[42]

The introduction of new suggestions, usually by Socrates, is an extremely common form of transition to further discussion.[43] Sometimes the argument is led on by a series of such suggestions.[44] Various transitional phrases, formulas and particles are used to preface them.

---

[42] The above analysis will illustrate not only the use of dichotomy, but also Plato's method of advancing from point to point in an induction.

[43] Cf. pp. 92 f. for a literary elaboration of this method of transition.

[44] Cf. Phil. 26e seq., 31b seq.

The formulas of command and exhortation noted above,[45] and similar phrases bespeaking the attention[46] are regularly used to introduce new suggestions. So in Protag. 324a the phrase εἰ γὰρ ἐθέλεις ἐννοῆσαι, introduces Protagoras' views on punishment. Similarly the command τῷ δὲ δὴ ἐντεῦθεν ἤδη πρόσσχες τὸν νοῦν introduces the discussion of the arithmetician in Theaet. 198b.

The introductory formula often takes the form of a question as to the agreement of the respondent.[47] So in Theaet. 189e, the definition of thought as conversation of the soul with herself is introduced by the query τὸ δὲ διανοεῖσθαι ἆρ' ὅπερ ἐγὼ καλεῖς. A new term or idea is sometimes introduced by the abrupt question whether it is included in the respondent's vocabulary, whether he recognizes its existence.[48] The subject thus introduced often seems entirely irrelevant. So in Rep. 349d, the subject of music introduced in this way, μουσικὸν δέ τινα λέγεις, ἕτερον δὲ ἄμουσον, seems at first sight to have nothing to do with the argument. However, it serves as the starting-point for a refutation of Thrasymachus drawn from the analogy of the arts.

One of the commonest methods of opening a discussion or making a fresh start in an argument is by demand for a definition.[49] The demand may be introduced in various ways. In Euthyphro the dramatic explanation of the benefit to Socrates from becoming a pupil of the pious Euthyphro (5a-c) and the generalization of the idea of piety (5d) lead up to the request for a definition which starts the discussion. (5d). In Euthyphro 11b the formula ἀλλὰ πάλιν εἰπὲ ἐξ ἀρχῆς introduces the reiteration of the request and consequent fresh start in the argument. Again in 15c a similar transition appears, reinforced

---

[45] Cf. *supra*, pp. 53 f. Akin to the formula of exhortation is the interrogative formula with βούλει and the subjunctive. Cf. Phil. 11b where Socrates introduces an explicit statement of the question at issue with the words βούλει συγκεφαλαιωσώμεθα ἑκάτερον. Also Protag. 317d; Laches 193e, 194b; Meno 76c, 86c; Phil. 28e; Rep. 521c, 577b; Theaet. 199a; Crat. 383a; Phaedo 70b, 79a, 104c.

[46] Cf. Phil. 24e, 29a; Symp. 177b; Theaet. 201d; Meno 82b; Euthyph. 11e. See also pp. 67 f.

[47] Cf. Theaet. 189b-c; Phil. 31b, 38e; Phaedr. 268a; Phaedo 64c, 103c; similarly Rep. 456d; 434a.

[48] Cf. Gorg. 454c, 464a; Theaet. 163e, 198a; Protag. 332a; Phaedo, 103c, d; Crat. 385b; I Alc. 128 b; Soph. 226b; Meno 75e, 76a, c, d, 88a; Rep. 352d; 348c. These same formulas are also used to introduce a definition of terms; so in Protag. 358c d; Theaet. 145d; Phil. 34e, 37a; Phaedo 64c.

[49] Cf. Phil. 13b; Theaet. 146c, 148d, 151d, 187b, 200d; Char. 159a, 160d; Laches 190d, 191e, 194c; Lysis 212a; Gorg. 449d; Meno 71d, 72c, 86c.

by the appropriate image of Proteus. As Euthyphro refuses to exert himself further the dialogue comes to a conclusion.

There are several types of transition in which the idea of criticism or correction is the prominent element. One such has already been noted.[50] The criticism may take the form of a demand for greater clearness which serves to introduce discussion or explanation.[51] So in Rep. 332c the request for a more specific definition, developed and illustrated through the analogy of the arts, leads to an explanation of terms which provokes discussion. Similarly, in Protag. 318b-c, Socrates' criticism of the vague reply of Protagoras, supported by analogous examples, leads to a more adequate response which is capable of being discussed. The demand for clearness may come from Socrates, as in the examples noted above, or it may be consequent upon the respondent's failure to understand some statement. His request for more exact explanation of a point not sufficiently clear is a frequent method of introducing concrete illustration or detailed exposition. The uses and varieties of this type of transition will be discussed further[52] in connection with its literary value. Its characteristic vocabulary includes imperative formulas such as λέγε μόνον, φράζε σαφέστερον, and interrogative formulas such as ποῖον δὴ λέγεις; πῶς λέγεις.[53] The criticism may take the form of a question as to the adequacy of some statement or its relevance to the present discussion.[54] So in Phil. 17e-18a Philebus praises Socrates' discourse on method, but demands what its application is to the problem in hand.[55] In Meno 75c Meno's objecton to Socrates' definition of figure serves as the transition to a short digression on the difference between dialectic and eristic.

Another common method of advancing the argument is through generalization. In the search for definition it often serves as the transition from a failure to further attempts on the respondent's part. The generalization is frequently introduced by some words of praise or excuse to soften the following criticism. So in Rep. 331c Socrates

---

[50] Cf. *supra*, p. 55.
[51] Cf. Protag. 312d, 320b-c; Phil. 37a; Euthyph. 6c d.
[52] Pp. 87 ff.
[53] Laws 691b, 700a; Phaedr. 257e, 261e, 263a; Phil. 14c, 17a, 23e, 25d, 31e, 51b, d, 53d, e; Theaet. 155d.
[54] Cf. Meno 73d, 78d, 79c, 97d; Theaet. 169de.
[55] Cf. pp. 89 ff. for a different combination of praise and criticism in transition.

compliments the aged Cephalus on his excellent words before he generalizes them into a definition of justice and proceeds to test their adequacy. The generalization in this case forms a transition to the testing by negative instances, and to consequent further discussion.

In Laches 191e, the generalization follows the testing and rejection of Laches' first definition of courage, and serves as the transition to his second attempt. Here, however, owing to Laches' inability to grasp the meaning of a general concept, Socrates is obliged to give him the further assistance of a sample definition (192a b); thus an additional element enters into the transition. Socrates prefaces the generalization with a word of apology for his own unskilful questioning to which he attributes Laches' failure. With this passage in the Laches, it is interesting to compare Laws 633c, where a similar generalization of courage is used as a transition.[56]

A generalization may be developed as a conclusion from several particular instances or it may serve as the basis for a conclusion through application to a particular instance. It is interesting to note how such shifts from particular to general and from general to particular[57] are effected. In Protag. 327c the transition from general to particular is made by the application to the inquiry about virtue of a general analogy drawn from the arts. The phrase οὕτως οἷον καὶ νῦν marks the application. Various combinations of deictic adverbs and inferential phrases and particles are similarly used; e.g., διὰ τί οὖν; καὶ νῦν δή, τοῦτο αὖ μάθε, οὐκοῦν and the elliptical ἐπεί.[58] Laches 185d illustrates the establishment of a general conclusion from several particular instances. οὐκοῦν ἑνὶ λόγῳ introduces the generalization. A slighter instance of this shift appears in Theaet. 175c where the generalizing phrase περὶ τούτων ἁπάντων gathers up a long list of details. The adverb συλλήβδην is another word characteristic of this form of transition.[59]

[56] Cf. Euthyph. 5d; Theaet. 178a. Theaet. 147d-148b is interesting as an exercise in generalization.
[57] In Theaet. 190b, particular, general and particular follow one another in the a b a order.
[58] Cf. Laches 183c, 185e, 189e; Protag. 326e; Symp. 205d; Phaedr. 238b; Meno 71b, 87e; Euthyph. 12a; Rep. 346a, 353d.
[59] Cf. Theaet. 155c, 193b, 175b, 196b; Meno 73bc, 85c, 88c; Phaedr. 238b, 247e, 249e; Phil. 29d, 32a, 50b; Protag. 325c; Rep. 335d, 342e, 350a, 353d; Laches 192b; Lysis 215d; Char. 167d; Gorg. 476d; Phaedo 66b; Euthyph. 13c.

MINOR FORMS OF TRANSITION

The constant appeal to analogous illustrations is a common characteristic of the Socratic method of reasoning. Their employment in making the shift from general to particular[60] is only one instance of their appearance in the dialogues. They occur so often that it seems worth while to make a further study of the transitional phrases used in their introduction and application. The introductory transitional reference to the illustration may be very explicit, as in the phrase σμικρὸν λαβὲ παράδειγμα and similar phrases;[61] more often a phrase with ὥσπερ or οἷον is used,[62] or an introductory αὐτίκα, οὐκοῦν, οὖν or elliptical ἐπεί.[63] In introducing further illustrations[64] or examples, when one has been already given, the adverbs καί, ἔτι, αὖ and the prepositional phrases πρὸς and ἐπὶ τούτοις appear in various combinations.[65] The mechanical phrase εἰ δὲ βούλει is similarly used.[66] In marking the transition to the application of an illustration or example the deictic adverb οὕτω is frequently used combined with some connective or inferential particle, e.g., οὕτω δή, οὕτω καὶ νῦν, οὕτω δὲ καί, οὕτω τοίνυν;[67] less stereotyped phrases are also common, so εἰς ταῦτα ἀποβλέπων in Protag. 320b; πρὸς τί οὖν δὴ λέγω ταῦτα, Meno 97e.[68]

To keep the machinery of the dialogues in motion a multitude of minor conventional phrases and particles of transition is necessary.

---

[60] Cf. *supra*, p. 64.
[61] Cf. Theaet. 154c, 176e; Soph. 218d.
[62] ὥσπερ, Phil. 18a; Phaedr. 265e; ὥσπερ τόδε, Symp. 205b; ὥσπερ οὖν εἰ, Protag. 334d; οἷον, Theaet. 147c, 175e, 207a, 208d; Phaedr. 240b; Euthyph. 13ab; Symp. 181a; Meno 73e, 86e; Phil. 29b; Crat. 387a; Phaedo 81e; Gorg. 495e.
[63] αὐτίκα, Protag. 359e; Theaet. 166b; Phaedr. 235e; Gorg. 483a. οὖν, οὐκοῦν, Phil. 31e; Crat. 388a, c, 390b; ἐπεί, Protag. 319e; Symp. 208c, d; Euthyph. 4c, 5e; Euthyd 307a; Laches 183c; ἐπεὶ αὐτίκα, Laches 195b.
[64] For further discussion of transitions in a series cf. *infra*, p. 66.
[65] οὐκοῦν καί, Symp. 199d; Meno 90d, 94a; Gorg. 477b; Theaet. 172a, 158d; Euthyph. 10a, c; Crat. 387b. ἐπεὶ καί, Phaedr. 344c; Theaet. 153a, 157a; Symp. 188a; Phil. 14d, 55a. ἔτι τοίνυν; ἔτι οὖν; Symp. 188b, 199e, 216a, 220e; Meno 88a; Phil. 47d, 51e; Phaedr. 240a; Protag. 326b; Theaet. 153c. Phrases with πρὸς and ἐπί; Phil. 20b, 37c, 23d, 55b; Theaet. 153c; Symp. 184e; Rep. 363e; Protag. 326b.
[66] Cf. Protag. 320a; Symp. 177b, 209d, 220d; Meno 94b.
[67] Cf. Protag. 334d, 347e; Theaet. 153d, 207b; Symp. 181a, 184c, 186c, 202b; Meno 72c, 87b; Phaedr. 245d; Phil. 18b.
Cf. also νῦν τοίνυν Meno 90e; ταὐτὸν δὲ τοῦτο καί; Symp. 178e, Pol. 287c.
[68] Cf. Phil. 34c, Char. 154b, Euthyph. 12c.
In Crat. 388d a transitional εἶεν introduces the application of a series of inductive examples to the case in hand.

Some of these are purely mechanical, with no inherent transitional meaning, such as the phrase εἰ δὲ βούλει noted above;[69] others are by nature connective, e.g., the numerous inferential phrases and particles. An adequate treatment of transitional particles would involve a careful analysis of many minor distinctions in usage and shades of meaning[70] which is far beyond the scope of the present paper. The following very incomplete collection of examples of some of the more obvious and general types of transitional phrases and particles will illustrate the possibilities for investigation along this line. In this discussion the material considered has been grouped under these headings: 1) transitional phrases and particles used in enumeration; 2) inferential phrases and particles used to mark some slight advance in the argument; 3) interrogative transitional phrases; 4) miscellaneous adverbial and prepositional phrases and particles of connection; 5) narrative phrases and formulas of transition.

In marking the transitions from point to point in an enumeration Plato uses not only the regular phrases πρῶτον, δεύτερον, τρίτον,[71] etc., but various other expressions as well. Often the first step is introduced by πρῶτον and further steps by simple variants such as εἶτα, ἔπειτα, αὖθις or αὖ;[72] or the introductory phraseology of the whole series may be varied from the conventional numerical expressions. αὐτίκα, ἑξῆς, ἔτι, μὲν–δέ, forms of ἄλλος, prepositional phrases such as μετὰ τοῦτο and ἐπὶ τούτοις, the phrase εἰ δὲ βούλει[73] and other similar expressions may be used.[74] The long speech of Nicias in Laches 181e–182e affords a good example of the skilful management of transitions in enumeration. The following is the series: πολλαχῆ, μὴ ἄλλοθι . . . ἀλλ' ἐν τούτῳ, καὶ ἅμα, ἔπειτα, μέγιστον μέντοι, ἔτι δὲ καί, προσθήσομεν δ' αὐτῷ οὐ σμικρὰν προσθήκην, μὴ ἀτιμάσωμεν δὲ εἰπεῖν. Word, phrase and sentence transitions are included. Finally a summarizing and dismissive μὲν οὖν brings the speech to a conclusion and a following δέ introduces the speech of Laches.

[69] Cf. *supra*, p. 65.
[70] This has been done for the particle γάρ by Geneva Misener, (University of Chicago Press, 1904)
[71] Cf. Phaedr. 266de, 271ab; Phil. 27b; Theaet. 193ab; 155ab; Rep. 358c.
[72] Cf. Phil. 15b, 21bc; Meno 90a, 95a; Symp. 181b, c, 184a, 189de, 207b, 210a, 211a, 219e-220a, 221ab, 222a; Theaet. 194d, 199d; Laches 186a.
[73] Cf. *supra*, p. 65 for discussion of transitions in a series of illustrations.
[74] Phil. 12cd, 18bc; Meno 71e, 92a, 93b-94b; Symp. 207de; Theaet. 166b; Laches 182e-183c, 191d-e; Gorg. 491b-c.

The inferential particles δή, οὖν, οὐκοῦν, ἄρα, and τοίνυν are constantly[75] used in transition, either alone or in combination with other particles and phrases. The use of μὲν οὖν, μὲν δή and μὲν τοίνυν in dismissals has been noted.[76] οὖν, μὲν οὖν and δή are also frequently used with resumptive force.[77] The common idiomatic μὲν οὖν which marks a correction[78] is of course transitional; so is the οὖν or δ' οὖν which waives further consideration of some point.[79] An inferential δή or οὖν combined with the adverb οὕτως may introduce a summary.[80] Inferential particles are often attached to an imperative. The introductory formulas of command with verbs of investigation discussed above[81] usually contain an inferential δή or οὖν. This construction is widely extended. Forms from εἰμι, ἔχω or any verb which may serve to attract the attention are used.[82] These brief quasi-exclamatory

[75] Their use with simple inferential force to mark some slight advance in the argument is so common as scarcely to need illustration. Cf. Symp. 178e, 180a, e, 181b, c, 183e, 201b, 207a, 208b; Meno 79ab, 87d, 90b; Phil. 21d, 26b, e, 40c, 49d; Protag. 330d; Euthyph. 7e, 13b, 14c; Phaedo 109a; Theaet. 170a, 185b; Phaedr. 244d, 261c, 262b et passim. ἄρα is constantly used to mark a conclusion; cf. Crat. 388b, e; Lysis 212d, 214d; Laches 186a; Protag. 332b, e, 340d; Theaet. 160cd; Rep. 350b; et passim.

[76] Cf. *supra*, pp. 56 ff.

[77] Char. 157b; Phil. 20a, 24d, 28a; Symp. 177c, 181a, e, 186e, 201d, 207a; Phaedr. 243b, 230e, 259d; Protag. 359b, 329b; Rep. 350d; Soph. 249b.

[78] Protag. 309d, 349e; Theaet. 165a, 181d; Symp. 201c, 202b; Phil. 25b, 39c; Phaedr. 234d; Laches 192c; Crat. 405a; Euthyd. 284b; Crito 44b; Rep. 341a, 392b, 444b.

[79] Phaedr. 230e, 253e, 260d; Laws 739e; Rep. 337c, 620d.

[80] Cf. Symp. 180b, 181a, 184a; Phaedr. 245d, 241e; Meno 88e; Pol. 301c; Rep. 556c.
For another transitional use of the same expression cf. *supra*, p. 65.

[81] Cf. *supra*, pp. 53 f.

[82] ἔχε δή Theaet. 186b; Laches 198b; Protag. 349e; Rep. 353b; Gorg. 460a, 490b. φέρε δή Crito 47a; Soph. 229b, 261d; Pol. 267a; Rep. 453e; Gorg. 493d; Protag. 330b, 332c, 349e; Meno 75b, 82d; Euthyd. 293b; Theaet. 203c, 206c, 209b; Phaedo 79b; Crat. 385 b; Phil. 27c. ἴθι δή, Theaet. 148d, 178b, 203b; Laches 194c, e; Gorg. 495c; Phaedr. 262d; Meno 77a; Phil. 11d; 27d; Protag. 332d, 333b, 352e, 359c; Crat. 389a; Hipp. II 368a; Pol. 305b; Rep. 399e, 455b. ἴθι οὖν, Rep. 376d; Symp. 199c; ἴθι οὖν δή, Theaet. 195e; ἴθι νῦν, Euthyph. 9a. ὅρα δή, Phaedo 79e; Euthyph. 12d; Theaet. 197c, 203c; Protag. 339b; Rep. 416d. ἄγε δή, Phil. 39e; Soph. 235a. Compare also the more explicit phrase πρόσεχε δὴ τὸν νοῦν and its variants, Meno 82b; Char. 160d; Phil. 31d, 32e, 45d; Symp. 210e, 217b; Theaet. 198b; Soph. 262e; Pol. 259d, 306c; Lysis 219b; Laws 667a.

phrases may be used alone to introduce a point or they may simply precede and reinforce a regular formula of command or exhortation. Interrogative transitional formulas with τί are very common. τί δέ; τί δή; τί οὖν; τί δὲ δή; τί δὴ οὖν; and other combinations occur.[83] They are used to mark any slight advance in the argument; to introduce an objection, a new suggestion, an illustration, or the application of some point. Formulas with πῶς and forms of ποῖος are also used.[84]

The importance of adverbs as an element in various forms of transition has already been sufficiently illustrated.[85] The adverbs οὕτως, ὧδε, αὖ, αὖθις, πάλιν, ἑξῆς, ἔτι, ἤδη all have transitional force. The exclamatory εἶεν, which is also transitional may for convenience be included here.[86] Here too should be noted the resumptive εἶτα, ἔπειτα or οὕτως which picks up and summarizes a list of participles.[87] Demonstratives always have transitional value. Transitions are often made by means of demonstratives alone or by phrases with the demonstrative pronouns. μετὰ τοῦτο and μετὰ ταῦτα are especially common,[88] either appearing alone or in some transitional formula. Similar phrases with ἐκ, διά, πρός, κατά, and περί are also used.[89] The transitional πρὸς or ἐπὶ τούτοις has already been noted.[90]

---

[83] τί δέ, Laches 185e, 192d, 195e, 199a; Meno 71c, 73a, 76a, 77e, 92e, 93e, 98b; Symp. 201b, 206a; Euthyph. 4a, 8b; Rep. 332e, 515b, 517d; Theaet. 148c, 153b, 154a, 205b; Protag. 332c, 351b, 353a, 356e; Phaedr. 234e, 258b; Phil. 11d, 22a, 29c, 40e; Phaedo 59c, 64d; Gorg. 478d, 495c. τί δή; Protag. 351c, 360d; Theaet. 204a; Gorg. 486e; τί οὖν; Char. 154e; Protag. 317d, 331a, 360c; Rep. 437b, 516c; Laches 193e; Meno 95b; Phil. 38e, 41e, 53b; Phaedr. 242d; 263c; Theaet. 154c, 158d, 164c, 168d, 200d; Gorg. 498a. τί δὲ δή; Protag. 358b,c; Theaet. 204b; Meno 87d, 95b; Euthyph. 14a; Phaedo 58c, 65a; Rep. 468a, 523e; Gorg. 502b. τί δ' αὖ; Theaet. 206a; Gorg. 504c. τί δὴ αὖ; Euthyph. 14c. τί δὴ οὖν; Rep. 369e; Gorg. 515e; Symp. 205a, 206e; Meno 89d; Euthyph. 10d.

[84] Cf. Phaedo 73d, 89c, 104d; Euthyd. 284c, 293e; Meno 91c, 96e; Laches 193e; Gorg. 491d; Phil. 11d, 13b, d, e, 14d, 21d, 29a, 24e, 31c, 35c, 36c, 39e and see Appendix, p. 103.

[85] Cf. supra, pp. 53, 57, 58 f., 63.

[86] Cf. Chap. I, pp. 29, 42, 44; also Crat. 388d; Laws 690, 691b; Gorg. 472d, 480a; Apol. 18e, 19b; Symp. 176a; Crito 47c; Meno 75c, 78d, 83c; Char. 156a; Phaedo 95a; Phil. 15d, 25b, 27e; Rep. 332d, e, 350d, 353b, 412b; et al.

[87] Cf. Theaet. 193c; Protag. 319d, 358c; Rep. 331b, 336e, 443e, 591e.

[88] Cf. Protag. 311a, 313a, 325d, 330d, e, 344b, 355a; Theaet. 148a; Rep. 456c; Meno 72c, 87c; Euthyph. 12d; Phaedo 102b; Phil. 29d, 38c, 52d; Symp. 175c, 176a, e, 197c, 199c, 204d, 210b, 215b, 219e et passim.

[89] Cf. Protag. 326a; Lysis 218a; Gorg. 454b; Phaedo 58c, 59a, 66b, d, 67e, 74a; Rep. 408c; Symp. 180b, 184a, 198e; Phil. 29e, 57c, et al.

[90] Cf. supra, p. 65.

The phrases ἐξ ἀρχῆς and εἰς αὖθις have also been discussed.[91] Phil. 52d is interesting as an illustration of the frequent piling up of transitional phrases and adverbs in one minor transition. ἔτι τοίνυν πρὸς τούτοις, μετὰ ταῦτα, τόδε αὐτῶν διαθετέον. τὸ ποῖον;

The ordinary connective usages of καί, μέν-δέ and ἀλλά do not need illustration, but there are several idiomatic transitional uses of these particles, alone and in combination with others, which may be noted. E.g., καὶ δὴ καί is used to apply a general statement to a particular case or introduce emphatically an important point;[92] γε alone or with δή or καί may indicate the transition to a new class;[93] δέ γε is regularly used to mark a minor premise;[94] δέ is used to pick up and define a term already introduced;[95] ἀλλὰ μήν, ἢ καί, ἢ καί and καὶ μήν may mark the advance to a new point, or a slight step forward in the argument.[96] ἀλλὰ γάρ and ἀλλὰ δή are used to introduce an objection or its answer.[97]

The narrated dialogues furnish countless examples of the various common transitional formulas with ἔφη, εἶπον, ἀκούω and similar verbs, which are essential to that type of writing.[98] In a well-known passage in the Theaetetus[99] Plato himself lists some of these phrases.

[91] Cf. *supra*, pp. 54, 58.
[92] Cf. Meno 70b, 88d, 89e; Phil. 12e; Laches 182d; Euthyph. 2d; Theaet. 171d, 187c; Symp. 182a; Protag. 339a, 343b, 345e; Rep. 328e, 343b, 373a, 420d et al.; Phaedo 59d, 85d.
[93] Cf. Rep. 425b; Theaet. 156b; Gorg. 450d.
[94] Cf. Rep. 335d, 349c, 412d; Theaet. 204e; Meno 84e; Gorg. 498e.
[95] Cf. Symp. 186d, 207d; Phil. 11c; Phaedr. 246d, 247c; Meno 86e; Theaet. 176b; Laches 198b; Euthyph. 10c; Phaedo 68a; Rep. 444d. Cf. also δὲ δή in Phaedr. 238a; and γάρ in Euthyph. 2d; Laches 198b.
[96] καὶ μήν Phaedo 71a, 72e; Gorg. 471d; Laws 629b, 640a; Rep. 370e, 424a, 431d; Laches 181a, 193c, 199e; Euthyph. 12a; Theaet. 143e, 148b, 149c, 153b, 159a, 170d, 182e, 188a, 204d; Meno 87d, 98c; Symp. 179b, 196c, 202b, 199c; Phil. 17b, 18e, 21c, 26a,d, 27a, 31a, 33c, 48a, *et passim*. καὶ μήν is sometimes slightly adversative in tone like καί τοι. ἀλλὰ μήν Rep. 370b, 468c, 502b, 525a; Phil. 35b; Phaedr. 240a, 244d; Symp. 176d; Protag. 332a, 359d, 360c; Theaet. 188e, 189a, 190d; Crat. 386d; Phaedo 74c, 75a. ἢ καί Protag. 330a; Euthyph. 8c; Theaet. 149a, 178b, 184e, 186a, 188e; Phaedo 76b; Rep. 348d.
[97] Cf. Protag. 338c; Theaet. 176b; Euthyph. 6d; Meno. 94d, e; Rep. 365cd, 487b; Symp. 199a; Laws 805b; Rep. 366a; Phil. 43a, 49c. Cf. also ἀλλά in Meno 75c; ἀλλὰ μήν Symp. 202d.
[98] Cf. Symp. 174c, 175b, 176e, 185c, 198a, 208b, 212c, 218d, 219a, 222c; Char. 156d; Protag. 318b, 330b, 339b, d, 337a, c, 340e, 347b; Phaedo 69e, 73a; Rep. 336b, d, 337a *et passim*.
[99] Theaet. 143c.

Besides these formulas with verbs of saying, the common continuative particles, οὖν, μὲν οὖν, δή, γάρ, καί, μέν, δέ, ἀλλά and the conjunctions and adverbs which indicate time sequence, such as ἐπεί, ἐπειδή, δῆτα, ἤδη, are naturally used with special frequency to mark transitions in narrative.[100]

[100] Cf. Char. 153a-d, 155b; Symp. 174a, 175b, 176ab, 177a-e, 180d, 189c; Protag. 318a, 320c seq., 342a, 310a; Phaedo 59d-e; Rep. 614b-621b, *et passim*.

CHAPTER III

THE LITERARY ART OF TRANSITION

Plato is the first great artist of prose style. He resembles the cleverest modern writers in his complete mastery over his material and his ready command of every device for securing unity and variety. This skill is nowhere more apparent than in his management of transitions. In Plato's hands transition becomes a literary art. Not only does he understand how to use to the best advantage the ordinary conventional means of connection, the formulas of summary and dismissal, the explicit statement of purpose, the multitude of transitional phrases and particles which are the natural resource and the common property of other ancient writers; but he is master also of the use in transition of image, proverb, quotation, continued metaphor; he is aware of the artistic value for purposes of transition of literary devices such as the ironic self-check, the paradox, dramatic personification of the argument, and he is not afraid to play with the order of the subject for the sake of gaining variety and heightening interest.

The use of literary allusion or adapted quotation in transition seems preëminently modern. But in Symp. 220c through an adapted Homeric quotation[1] Plato secures real literary value for an otherwise ordinary dismissive-introductive transition. "I have told you one tale, but another instance is worth hearing of the deeds and endurance of that mighty man, while he was on the expedition." Different but equally modern is the passage in the Phaedrus (243a) where the reference to Stesichorus and quotation from his palinode form the chief step in transition to the idea of a second speech from Socrates in recantation of his first. What seems like a playful whim or capricious impulse is really studied art, a clever literary method of securing an effective transition from a superficial and inadequate treatment of love to one that is deeper and more complete.[2] Another

---

[1] Od IV-242.
[2] See p. 21.

interesting element in this paragraph of transition is Socrates' use of proverbial language in the explicit statement of purpose which closes his brief summary of his reasons for recantation. "I desire as it were to wash the brine from my ears with water from the spring."[3]

In Lysis 213e–214b an appeal to the authority of the poets is combined with metaphor in advancing to a new point in the discussion. The transitional formula of exhortation, "But let us proceed no further in this direction," suggests the noun-metaphor of the hard road of investigation. The language of this metaphor continues, leading up to the reference to the poets. And here another metaphor, the description of the poets as "fathers and leaders in wisdom," adds further variety before the actual quotation[4] which starts the new discussion. This transition then includes formula, image and literary reference.

A recurrent metaphor used in transition may be an important element in the literary frame work of a dialogue. So in the Republic the figure of the "sea of difficulty," first casually introduced in a dismissive transitional formula in 441c,[5] appears again with greater elaboration in 453d in transition to a refutation of the charge of inconsistency. It is further developed into the figure of the three waves of ridicule in 457bc where it serves as the transition from the first paradox, the community of education between male and female guardians to the second, the community of wives and children for the guardians. After much postponement and digression, it is used again in 472a to introduce the discussion of the possibility of the third paradox, the rule of philosopher-kings. Finally in 473c the metaphor of the "laughing wave" prefaces the actual statement of the third paradox which in 472 was postponed by a brief digression on the relation of the ideal to the actual. This image then not only helps to give artistic unity to Book V but, if we accept 441c as a preparatory hint, links this book to the preceding.

[3] The probable literary source of this expression is Od. 6:224, as has been pointed out by Shorey in *The English Classical Review*, 1904, p. 302 f.

[4] Od. XVII 218.

[5] Campbell (*Republic*, Vol. II, p. 12) finds the first hint even earlier, in ἐμπεπτώκαμεν, 435c. Shorey, (*A. J. P.*, XVI 225) rejects as fanciful any discovery of the image of the wave in these passages (435c and 441c). At the best, in his opinion, they are "unconscious anticipations."

The above description of instances of artistic transition is sufficient to show how any attempt at classification is beset with difficulties. In the majority of cases where the transition has any literary value it is not simple but complex, a skilful combination of a number of transitional elements. It may be that one element is so evidently predominant that the transition easily falls under one category. On the other hand, several elements may seem equally important. The classification followed in this chapter, is purely tentative, adopted for convenience of discussion, not intended to be either definitive or exhaustive.

Other Greek writers quote proverbs; Plato is the first to incorporate a proverb in his argument so that it becomes the link of transition from one point to the next. In Rep. 423c-e where Socrates and Adeimantus are discussing the injunctions to be laid upon the guardians, transition is made by means of a proverb[6] to the idea that, if only the guardians receive the proper education and nurture, "the one great thing," then the "many" minor details of legislation may safely be left to them. Similarly in Laches 196d by means of the proverb, "not every pig would know," to which he adds the words, "nor be courageous," Socrates passes to the point that, according to the definition of Nicias, courage must be denied to animals.[7] Euthydemus 297c presents an entertaining variation of this method. The sophist accuses Socrates of running away and refusing to answer. He retorts with the proverb that "not even Hercules could fight agains two," which he proceeds to explain and adapt playfully to the present case. But the sophist, in no wise abashed, picks up the reference to the proverb and uses it to continue the game of eristic quibbles.[8]

In Phaedo 99c a proverb is used in combination with a transition of the ordinary dismissive-introductive type. The failure of Socrates to find the final cause is dismissed with μὲν οὖν; the narrative then advances with a continuative δέ; but it is the following proverbial

---

[6] The proverb is πολλ' οἶδ' ἀλώπηξ ἀλλ' ἐχῖνος ἓν μέγα. Adam's edition of the *Republic* notes the reference to proverbial language, but does not cite the proverb. Other editors seem to have missed the meaning of τὸ λεγόμενον here. The same proverb is similarly used in Pol. 297a.

[7] See also Phaedr. 257d; Phaedo 108d; Pol. 264b; Lysis 207c; Phil. 48c.

[8] See also Phaedo 89c and Laws 919b for use of this proverb.

expression "τὸν δεύτερον πλοῦν"[9] that really supplies the main element of transition to the theory of ideas and method of hypotheses. In many similar cases of transition by other methods a proverb appearing at the point of transition attracts the attention and adds emphasis. So in Phaedrus 260c, the transition is very effectively reinforced by a proverb. The amusing illustration of the man who, deceived by an ignorant but eloquent friend, purchases an ass in the belief that it is a horse, is applied to the case of an orator who, himself ignorant of good and evil, deceives an equally ignorant city. The transition to the application is really made by the words "not about an ass." But these words at once suggest the proverb "The shadow of an ass." The adoption of the proverbial expression here adds to the effectiveness of the transition.[10]

A proverb brought in at the point where a change in speakers is made may add greatly to the smoothness and naturalness of the transition. Note for example the use of the proverb, "Let brother help brother," in Rep. 362d, and the expression "Your will is my will" in Theaet. 162b where Socrates returns to Theaetetus as respondent. Again in Crat. 411a in the transition to the explanation of the derivation of the names of the four virtues, the familiar[11] exhortation not to be discouraged gains a new emphasis from the addition of the proverbial phrase "put on the lion's skin."[12] Similarly, in Phil. 60a, the proverb "twice and thrice what is fair,"[13] in modified form reinforces the statement of the need of recapitulation which, set in a framework of minor transitional formulas, introduces another résumé and reminder of the issue.

The familiar proverb, "the third to the Savior," is frequently used by Plato in the introduction of the final stage in an argument or discussion. So in Char. 167ab where the regular formula, "Then let us investigate again as if from the beginning," serves as the transition

---

[9] Compare our expression, "the second best." This proverb is used also in Phil. 19c, Pol. 300c.

[10] Cf. also Laws 753e; Phil. 29a; Rep. 435c, 563d, 497d, 521c; Theaet 208b; Pol. 300c; Laws 723d, 701d, 968e; Lysis 218c; Phaedr. 272c; Theaet. 201d.

[11] Cf. p. 54.

[12] See also Soph. 261b where the proverb "such a faint heart will never take a city" is similarly used.

[13] This proverb is similarly used in Gorg. 498e in Socrates' appeal to Callicles for his help in drawing out the conclusions from their argument. See also Laws 754c, 956e.

to examination of the sixth definition of temperance, the proverb "the third to the Savior" inserted in the formula emphasizes the finality of the attempt and gives a literary value to the transition. Again, in Rep. 583b, this proverbial expression appears in combination with the figure of the Olympic contest to introduce the third and last argument for the superiority of the just over the unjust life. The use of the figure enhances the idea of finality suggested by the proverb. In this greatest of moral contests, as in the physical, it is the third throw that wins.[14]

Plato uses quotations in transition in several ways.[15] The quotation may serve to introduce a new character either in narrative or argument. The case in Protag. 315bc is especially apt. The lines which introduce the heroes Heracles and Tantalus in the eleventh book of the Odyssey (Od. XI, 601 and 582) are here adapted to preface the half-humorous descriptions of the famous sophists Hippias and Prodicus. Again in Protag. 340a it is by means of a Homeric quotation (Il. XXI, 308) that Prodicus is brought into the argument to assist Socrates. There is a somewhat similar use in Gorg. 505e, where a quotation from Epicharmus, "Two men spoke before, but now one shall be enough," introduces Socrates' consent to serve in the double capacity of questioner and respondent.

More frequent and important is the use of quotations in the progress of the argument to effect the transition from point to point in the discussion.[16] So in Charmides 173a an allusion to the passage in the Odyssey[17] describing the two gates of dreams forms the transition to the investigation whether temperance as a "science of sciences" would have any practical value. Two such cases of transitional use

[14] For further examples of the use of this proverb in transition see Phil. 66d, where it introduces the third recapitulation, and Laws 692a.

[15] The use of a proverb or a quotation to formulate a definition or a new point for debate can hardly be called transitional. Although the quotation or proverb in such cases does serve to indicate a new phase of discussion, the actual transition is usually found in some prefatory phrase or formula. See Meno 77b; Gorgias 510b; Char. 164d; Rep. 407ab; Euthyphro 12b; Laws 629, 630a–c, 731e. The common use of quotations in illustration or proof is also non-transitional. See Char. 163b; Gorgias 484b, 526d; Symp. 195d; Laches 201b; Lysis 215c; Laws 680b, 681e, 690e.

[16] Instances of this use of quotation in Rep. 545d, e, 547a, 550c; Crito 44b, have been described already in Chap. I, pp. 8, 43. See also Crat. 428a.

[17] Od. XIX 562.

of quotation occur in the Gorgias. The reference to the well-known drinking song in 451d introduces the idea that Gorgias' definition of rhetoric is inadequate, being praise not definition. Again, in 492e, a saying of Euripides[18] prefaces Socrates' explanation of the Pythagorean view that our body is our tomb.

A familiar quotation may be adapted as a transitional formula,[19] a minor connecting link in the train of thought. So in Meno 76d Socrates introduces his Gorgian definition of color with the words, "And now, as Pindar says,[20] read my meaning." The quotation here is combined with the inferential phrase ἐκ τούτων δή. Similarly in Rep. 563c a quotation from Aeschylus,[21] "Why not . . . utter the word which rises to our lips," is combined with οὐκοῦν to form a transition. Another possible instance is Crat. 428d. Here a Homeric quotation[22] is cleverly introduced into a transitional self-check.

Proverb and quotation occasionally appear together in a transition. So in Symp. 174b Socrates' punning adaptation of the proverb, "To the feasts of inferior men the good go unbidden," combined with playful criticism of Il. II 408 and another Homeric reference (Il. X 224)[23] are important transitional elements in the passage of by-play which serves as the introductory explanation of Aristodemus' presence at Agathon's banquet. Similarly the "subtly moralized" paraphrase of Hesiod (O. D. 293) which appears in Phil. 19c[24] involved with the proverbial expression, "τὸν δεύτερον πλοῦν" serves as the transition to the demand that Socrates shall undertake the enumeration and definition of the species of pleasure and wisdom, which Protarchus feels unable to attempt.

Plato's use of images in transition is even more varied than his use of proverb and quotation. In some cases the language of the transition is only slightly figurative or fanciful, suggesting metaphor, in others the figure is clearly developed and applied. Sometimes such a metaphor is extended over several pages; it may even appear as a

[18] Frag. 7 of the Polycides.
[19] For additional examples see Phaedr. 260a; Symp. 220c.
[20] Frag. 82.
[21] Frag. 351 Nauck.
[22] Il. III 109.
[23] The same quotation is used transitionally in II Alcib. 140a. Compare Protag. 348c where it is used by Socrates to support his claim of disinterestedness.
[24] Shorey, A. J. P. XIII, p. 372.

unifying element throughout the dialogue. In Rep. 427d the regular dismissive-introductive transition by which Socrates introduces the search for justice in the now completed ideal city, is varied by the addition of the words, "bringing a torch from somewhere," which give a figurative touch to the whole. So in Theaetetus 187b in a transition to a fresh start in the argument the ordinary transitional formula, "and now consider again from the beginning," is enlivened by the added figure, "having wiped out áll that went before."[25] In Theaetetus 164c as in 187b the image appears in conjunction with a conventional formula of transition to a fresh start in the argument. But the more fully developed metaphor of 164c, "Like a cock of mongrel breed we seem to have leaped away from the argument and begun to crow before we have won the victory," does more than add vigor and individuality to the transition. This striking figurative expression of the idea of mistaken confidence forms a natural and effective introduction to the criticism of the previous method of conducting the argument.

A figure may be used for climactic effect in a transitional series. So in Symp. 217e-218b, where Alcibiades prefaces an anecdote of Socrates by an enumeration of his reasons for relating it, the regular phraseology of the series[26] is employed, but it is the vigor and vividness of its imagery—detailed comparison of the effect of philosophy on the soul to the bite of a serpent, followed by the lesser figures of the philosophic madness and Bacchanalian frenzy—which makes the third reason an effective climax and the most important step in the transition.

In Rep. 403e, the comparison of the guardians to athletes of war is used in working out the conclusion that their gymnastic training must be "simple" and "not over-precise." The more specific transition to this subject is in the phrase τί δὲ δή; but the following words, "for are the men not in training for the greatest contest?" add a more important element, for the application of this figure colors the whole discussion.

An image may be used in the introduction of another personage into the dialogue or in making a shift of interlocutors. So in Theaet. 162b the implicit application to the present case of the Spartan

[25] Similarly the figure of "retracing our steps" gives artistic value to the transition in Theaet. 187e. See also Theaet. 200e; Laws 892d, 893b.
[26] See Chap. II, p. 66.

custom of compelling every one who enters the gymnasium to strip and display his skill in contest is pressed by Socrates and evaded by Theodorus with the result that Theaetetus again becomes the respondent. Again in 169a-b the shift to Theodorus is finally effected by a reference to this same simile of 162b and a further comparison of Socrates to Skiron and Antaeus. So also in Laches 194bc, when the elenchus has reduced Laches to perplexity, it is by means of the figures of the huntsmen and the storm that Nicias is introduced into the discussion.[27]

A figure may be employed as a formula,[28] as an external means of transition to a new line of investigation. An instance of this is the figure of the wrestler in Rep. 544b which introduces the return to the discussion of the types of degenerate states. "Then, like a wrestler . . . . you must put yourself again in the same position; and let me ask you the same questions, and do you give me the same answer which you were about to give me then." An even clearer case is the metaphor of the game of draughts used in transition in Laws 739a, "The next move in our pastime of legislation."

The transitions from point to point in the progress of an argument afford great opportunity for a varied use of metaphor. Transition to an objection or correction may be made through an image.[29] So in Theaet. 203d-e the comparison of the argument to a runaway slave introduces the correction, "Perhaps we ought to have maintained that a syllable is not the letters, but one single idea formed out of them." Rep. 458 a-b illustrates the literary elaboration of a postponement[30] by means of a figure. The discussion of the possibility of the second paradox involves the discussion of the possibility of the entire state. Socrates introduces the idea of postponement by the metaphor of the day-dreams of an indolent man, in the application of which he outlines the order he wishes to adopt. "So now I too shrink from the harder task, and I want to postpone those matters and consider later how they are possible," etc.

[27] Also Theaet, 184b.
[28] Compare also Phaedr. 236b; Pol. 287c; Phil. 13d, 41b, 44d.
[29] See also Theaet. 164c, 208e.
[30] In Symp. 209e–210a a dismissive-introductive transition is similarly embellished by a figure. Compare also Rep. 432b-d; Phil. 55c.

Personification of the argument is a type of metaphor rather frequently used in transition.[31] So in Phaedr. 260e Socrates employs the personified λόγοι to bear witness to the theory that rhetoric may be a mere unscientific knack, rather than an art. The figure is more elaborately developed in Theaet. 164e, where complaint against the maltreatment of the orphaned discourse of Protagoras and the failure of its natural protectors, such as Theodorus, to come to its assistance serves as a clever transition to the so-called "defence of Protagoras" by Socrates. The personification of the argument in Laches 194a involves a literary conceit.[32] After the failure of the definition of courage as endurance, Socrates, picking up and playing on the phraseology of the subject under consideration, makes abrupt transition to further discussion by the literary conceit of enduring at the bidding of the argument that courage may not laugh at their lack of courage in investigating her nature.

Although the figure in transition often seems a mere artistic substitute for or reinforcement of a conventional formula, it sometimes stands in a much more intimate relation to the argument. The new idea introduced may be implicitly suggested by the figure or developed by its direct application.[33] Thus in Rep. 343b it is through the figure of the shepherd and its application that transition is made from the ideal to practical experience in the consideration of justice and injustice. The paragraph of transition in Theaet. 179d illustrates both uses of metaphor. The first figure is incorporated in a transitional formula. "And therefore let us draw nearer . . . and give the truth of the universal flux a ring; is the theory sound or rotten?" The second figure, that of the war which is raging about the theory, contributes both language and ideas to the following discussion. In 181a it is used in transition again, combined with further figurative language, Socrates' comparison of their position to that of "players in the palaestra who are caught upon the line, and are dragged different ways by the two parties."

[31] Compare Theaet. 200c; Rep. 503a, 538d; Laws 699e, 701c, 892d; Phaedo 95a.

[32] Another example of a literary conceit used in transition occurs in Symp. 185c, where the usual transitional reference to the previous speaker takes the form of a Gorgian paronomasia.

[33] Compare Rep. 368d, 484c; Theaet. 155e, 167b; Gorg. 486d; Phil. 38e–39b; Laws 803ab; Phil. 59de; Laws 960cd.

There is a very clever instance of the use of an applied figure in transition in Meno 72a. After the enumeration of virtues which Meno offers as a definition, Socrates comments, "I certainly seem to have met with great good fortune, Meno, if, when seeking for one virtue, I have discovered a whole swarm of them which are in your keeping." Then picking up this image of the swarm he uses it in an illustration, introduced by ἀτάρ, put in the form of an imagined question whether bees differ "as bees." In this way he reaches the idea that a definition must give the essence or "common notion" of the thing defined. Again in Laws 734e–735a, the image of weaving the web, introduced by καθάπερ οὖν δή, suggests the idea of cleansing from which is developed the need of tests and purification in the state.

A case like that of the applied metaphor of the dog in Rep. 375 is sometimes criticized as fallacious. But the Republic is not a debate with an adversary nor is any argument in this instance based upon the metaphor. The image here is merely a literary device for illustrating the exposition of the temperament of the guardians. This is shown by 375d where a departure from the image is playfully alleged as the cause of their temporary bewilderment. "And I was at a loss, and when I had considered our previous words, I said, 'My friend it is with good right that we are in difficulty, for we have left the metaphor which we set before ourselves.'" Socrates then proceeds to further illustration through a return to the metaphor.[34]

The use of recurrent metaphor[35] is a feature of Platonic style which is often utilized in transition. Even when not strictly transitional its effect is always unifying; so in the Laches where the figure of the Doric harmony between a man's words and deeds introduced by Laches

---

[34] In some cases where transition is made by an image and its application, it is a subtlety of Platonic style to blend the image with the thing to which the image refers. This blending often results in a repetition of the phraseology of the image in the application, or a slightly strained adaptation to the image of the characteristics of the thing compared. The echoing of words and phrases recalls in outward semblance the Homeric simile. So in Rep. 402a–c where the figure of the letters and their images in water or in mirrors is applied to the forms of the virtues and their appearance in concrete shapes, the term εἰκόνας is used in both sides of the comparison, while the phrase οὔτ' ἐν σμικρῷ οὔτ' ἐν μεγάλῳ ἠτιμάζομεν αὐτά, used of the letters, seems framed especially to correspond to μήτε ἐν σμικροῖς μήτε ἐν μεγάλοις ἀτιμάζωμεν of the application.

[35] See George B. Hussey, *The More Complicated Figures of Comparison in Plato*, A. J. P., Vol. XVII, pp. 329–346.

in 188d is picked up by Socrates in 193d–e. The image of the φάρμακον by which Socrates characterizes the useful lie in Rep. 382c appears again in 389b, where its use is restricted to physicians and to the rulers. Later still, 459c, with a reference back to the earlier passage, it introduces the idea that the rulers must enforce proper regulations of marriage. Thus a new and important point is emphasized.[36]

In these simple cases the figure recurs but once or twice. In the longer dialogues one may find also more elaborate examples of this use of metaphor.[37] Bks. VIII and IX of the Republic contain a striking instance. The growing image of the drones in the hive plays an important part in binding together the descriptions of the degenerate states and the corresponding individuals. It is first[38] introduced in 552c in the description of the evils of oligarchy, where the idle spendthrift is compared to a drone. Socrates pauses here to elaborate the image by the distinction between the flying drones which are stingless and the walking drones which are both stinging and stingless. Through the further application of the developed figure he passes to the conclusion (552de) that paupers and criminals will be found together in the state. In 554bc drone-like desires, as of a pauper or rogue, are declared to exist in the oligarchical man. The figure reappears again in 555de in the description of the rise of democracy out of oligarchy. Ruined men of rank, ripe for conspiracy, and unscrupulous business men who reduce men to pauperdom by exorbitant rates of interest are both compared to stinging drones. The figure is used in 559c in pointing the difference between the democratic man and the oligarchical. Again, 559d, it is from the tasting of drone's honey that the change of the oligarchical principle into the democratic begins. In the account of the rise of tyranny out of democracy all the classes of the democratic state are described in terms of this figure; the idle spendthrifts who form the ruling power are drones (564b–d), the wealthy tradesmen are food for the drones 564e), and the people get their share of drone's honey (565a). Finally (565c), it is the drones' sting that drives men deprived of wealth to

[36] Similarly the figure of the "feast of reason" introduced in Rep. 352b is picked up in transition in 354a. Cf. pp. 34 f.

[37] The recurrent figure of the 'wave' in Rep. V has been described above, p. 72. See also Chap. I, p. 20 for reference to the recurrent metaphor of the defence in Phaedo 63b, d, e; 69d, e.

[38] The comparison of the state to a hive appears earlier (520b).

revolt and leads to the subsequent establishment of a tyranny. In 567d the tyrant's body-guard are described as drones. The figure recurs for the last time in the account of the nature and origin of the tyrannical man; in 573a, where the master-passion in his soul is described as a "monstrous winged drone"; in 574d, which describes the rise of this passion when pleasures begin to swarm in the hive of his soul; and in 577e, where the conclusion is reached that the tyrannical soul will be least of all able to do as it likes, being continually goaded by the sting of passion.[39]

The figure of the midwife in the Theaetetus is one of the most important examples of the recurrent transitional image. It appears frequently throughout the dialogue, sometimes alone, sometimes in combination with other methods of transition. The image is introduced first in 148e–149a, after Theaetetus' confession of his inability to define knowledge and his dissatisfaction at this failure. Through a long digression of dramatic dialogue and description, the figure is fully developed and in its entirety serves as the transition to renewed attempt at definition. In a narrower sense the resumptive formula and the familiar exhortation not to grow weary[40] with which the description closes (151d), mark the return from the digression to the argument. In 151e after the statement of the definition the formula, "But, come now, let us examine it together," reinforced by a reference to the metaphor, introduces the testing of the definition. In 157c–d the transition from puzzlement to continued effort on the part of Theaetetus is made by another recurrence to the metaphor and the ideas involved in its interpretation, the principle of Socratic ignorance and the method and purpose of the elenchus. In 160e, 161b, the figure of the midwife is combined with a new figure, that of the

[39] The figure of the drones in the hive is a subordinate comparison in the larger analogy of the state and the individual which extends as a framework throughout the Republic. See especially 368d, 434d–435e, 440b, 442de, 444a–e, 449a, 545b, 552c, 564b, 567c, 576a, 580c. Hussey, pp. 339 f. has worked out this analogy by diagrams. In its development a group of minor images, some of them recurrent, are used: the comparison of state and individual with the human body (401c, 409a, 591cd), especially in regard to health and disease (444d, 490c, 495d), with a harmony (401d, 430e, 432a, 591d), a ship (488, 573d), a beast (440b, 493ab, 572b, 588b, 591c), a bird's nest (548a, 573e), a many-colored cloak (557c, 558c, 561e). The references given above are not complete. See also Hussey, *loc. cit.*

[40] See p. 54.

ἀμφιδρόμια to introduce the testing of the definition that knowledge is perception, as interpreted and supported by the doctrines of Protagoras and the "flowing" philosophers. Again, in 184b, transition is made by means of reference to the image, to a fresh start in the argument and to the return to Theaetetus as respondent. Finally, in 210b, the image is employed to bring the dialogue to a conclusion.[41]

Hardly less important, though far less complicated, is the recurrent figure of the second prize in the Philebus. It appears first in 22c. Dismissing (with μὲν οὖν) the attempt to establish mind alone as the highest good, Socrates restates (with δὲ δή) in the form of this image of the second prize the modified view of the issue. Thus the transition is made to further investigation. In 23a the image is picked up, with δὲ δή, by Protarchus who agrees with Socrates as to the value of the discussion. In 33c the question whether the gods are or are not indifferent to pleasure is postponed by a reference to the image in a dismissive formula. Again in 61a, Socrates recurs to the main issue by means of this same image; "Then now we must ascertain the nature of the good more or less accurately, in order, as we were saying, that we may assign the second prize." And in 66e the image prefaces the final résumé and conclusion of the discussion.[42]

A trait that is sometimes missed by literary critics and translators of Plato is his use of recurrent figurative language or continued metaphor to lead up to and emphasize some moral idea. So in the Laws a figurative expression from the language of the Ideas, ποῖ βλέπων, repeated with minor variations of phraseology and grammar, constantly appears in connection with and leading up to the idea of the ethical aim of the law giver, which is itself one of the recurrent themes of the Laws.[43] A similar transitional use of musical terms occurs

[41] The Theaetetus contains an unusual number of recurrent metaphors; the image of the chorus, used in transition in 173bc; the wax tablet, 191cd, 194c, 200c; and the aviary 197c, 198d, 199a-e and 200c.

[42] Other cases of extended recurrent metaphor in the Laws, Timaeus and Politicus are treated by Hussey, pp. 343 ff. For another example of recurrent metaphor in the Philebus cf. Phil. 12bc, 22c, 26b, 28a.

[43] Laws 625e, πρὸς τοῦτο βλέπων; 626a, ἀποβλέπων εἰς; 630c, πρὸς τὴν μεγίστην ἀρετήν . . . βλέπων; 688a, πρὸς τοῦτο βλέποντα; 688b, πρὸς πᾶσαν μὲν βλέπειν; 687a, ποῖ βλέπων; 687b, πρὸς τοῦτο βλέπων; 693b, πρὸς ταῦτα βλέποντα; 707d, ἀποβλέποντες νῦν πρὸς . . . ἀρετήν; 714b, πρὸς ἀρετὴν . . . βλέπειν; 743c, ἐνταῦθα ἔβλεπεν; 757c, ἀποβλέποντας; 770c, πρὸς ταῦτα βλέποντας; 962a, οἷ βλέπειν δεῖ; 962d, πρὸς ἄλλο . . . βλέπει. See also 962e; 705d; 784a; 965b; 922e, et al.

in Laws 689 seq.;[44] the musical figure is kept up throughout the discussion of ignorance.

In this guidance of the thought by the choice of words the language is not necessarily figurative, nor is it always a moral tone that is thus secured.[45] Irony and a slightly hostile intention are shown by the persistent harping on πορίζομαι and its derivatives in Meno 78c–e. In Rep. 332 the constant repetition of ὀφειλόμενον, the word of the definition, emphasizes its inadequacy. A more important instance is the repetition of εὐχή in the third main division of the Republic (Bks. V–VII), by which Plato subtly hints his own recognition of the ideal and slightly chimerical character of his suggestions. The word occurs first in 450d in the introductory transition scene, where Socrates protests his "reluctance to approach the subject, lest our aspiration . . . should turn out to be a dream only." It is repeated in 456b, when the possibility of the community in education between the male and female guardians has been established. Again in 499c it recurs in a strong affirmation of the possibility and necessity of the rule of the philosopher-king. Finally in 540d, at the end of Bk.VII, it appears in a summarizing statement, "that what has been said about the state and the government is not a mere dream, and although difficult, not impossible."

Akin to the usage treated above is the frequent repetition, in widely separated parts of a dialogue, of some single word or phrase, which thus serves as a link of connection, subtle but psychologically strong.[46] So παρακαταθήκη which is prominent in Bk. I of the Republic (331 seq.) recurs after a long interval in Bk. IV 442e in the application of the common tests of justice to the city and individual just described.

When a recurrent phrase has emotional connotations it may be styled a leit-mitif. Such an artistic device seems at first sight purely ornamental, but is really unifying and transitional as well. The hint of the coming trial of Socrates appears as a leit-mitif in the Gorgias (511c, 521e and 522b) in the conversation of Socrates and Callicles

---

[44] 689a διαφωνίαν; 689b πλημμελεστάτας; 689d ἄνευ συμφωνίας; 691a διὰ πλημμέλειαν καὶ ἀμουσίαν.

[45] In Rep. 342 the importance of the idea of the ruler is emphasized by repetition.

[46] γηροτρόφον, Rep. 331a, is picked up in 569b. Compare also the repetition of ὑπεραποθνῄσκειν in Symp. 179b, 180a, 207b, 208d.

and yet more clearly in Meno 94e, 99e and 100c in the thinly veiled threats of Anytus and Socrates' references to his hostility. In the Euthyphro the trial is imminent and what was before a leit-motif is utilized in the development of the dramatic setting (Euthy. 2, 3, 15). A very impressive instance of the use of leit-motif occurs in the Phaedo. The words of Socrates in 61e referring to the impending discussion "For what else should one do in the time before sunset," repeated in substance if not in exact phraseology at the crisis of the argument in 89c, "Well, he said, summon me as your Iolaus, as long as it is still light," are echoed by Crito with almost intolerable pathos in the closing scene of the dialogue, (116e)—"But I think, said he, Socrates, that the sun is still shining upon the mountains, and that it has not yet set."[47]

The variety of ways in which Plato effects a transition by a single word is noteworthy. The use of a recurrent word in the guidance of the thought or as a unifying element has already been discussed. A figurative or poetic word is often used to arrest the attention and force the request for further explanation. Rep. 412e-413c illustrates this device. In making the statement that the guardians must be watched to see whether they constantly hold to their belief that they must act always to the best advantage of the city Socrates uses the poetic and figurative expressions γοητευόμενοι and ἐκβάλλουσι. Glaucon at once requests an explanation, picking up ἐκβάλλουσι in ἐκβολήν (412a). After satisfying him on this point Socrates repeats γοητευόμενοι with γοητευθέντες and introduces besides the metaphorical κλαπέντες. Glaucon is again completely mystified. Explanation follows. By this literary device Plato is enabled to elaborate an important idea and to impress it on the mind of the reader more surely than he could have done by pages of dogmatic exposition.[48]

A term which is to figure more or less prominently in later discussion may be introduced elaborately or casually into an earlier part of the discourse. So the term μέλλον which is introduced and defined in Theaet. 178a appears (in the form τῶν μελλόντων) in the latter part of b in an important new step in the argument. Similarly, in Theaet. 173e the verb ἀστρονομοῦσα which appears merely as one of many details in the description of the philosopher paves the way for the

[47] Compare also Phaedo 85b where the same idea occurs, though the phraseology is different.
[48] Compare εὐνάς in Rep. 415e.

typical illustrative anecdote of Thales the astronomer which follows in 174a. There is an important instance of this method of transition in Euthyphro 4e—where ὁσίου used by Euthyphro in the climax of his narrative is picked up by Socrates in τῶν ὁσίων and becomes the theme of inquiry for the remainder of the dialogue.[49]

A transition may be made by a play on words.[50] In Theaet. 171c, Theodorus protests against the rather invidious harping on "truth" with which Socrates concludes his half-serious refutation of Protagoras;—"We are running my friend too hard, Socrates." Socrates picks up the figurative καταθέομεν with another compound of θέω;—"But it isn't evident, my friend whether we are running beyond the truth," in transition to the assurance that he will not rely seriously upon the foregoing argument.

A word used literally may be picked up and applied in a figurative sense as in Char. 154e. Socrates has just given a moral turn to the conversation by the transition from body to soul. He now makes the transition to the idea of discussion by the suggestion, (introduced by τί οὖν) that they lay bare the soul of Charmides. The verb used is ἀπεδύσαμεν which repeats metaphorically the ἀποδῦναι of 154d. Similar in many respects, though set in a more complicated frame work, is the transition in Protag. 352ab. In an imaginary illustrative conversation dealing with the condition of the body, Socrates uses the word ἀποκαλύψας. Then by a shift from body to soul, he makes the application of the illustration to the mental attitude of Protagoras by repeating the verb in a figurative sense.

In most cases the repetition of the word involves no shift in meaning. So in Laches 181ab a short digression on the character of Socrates is introduced by καὶ μὴν and a repeated word. With ὀρθοῦντα Laches picks up the ὀρθοῖς in the speech of Lysimachus. There is a further echo in ὀρθή. The device may be repeated through several consecutive sentences forming a kind of "chain figure."[51] So in

[49] Compare Rep. 374d where φυλάκων first appears in the technical sense in which it is used throughout the Republic.

[50] In Laches 194d; Theaet. 180b; Rep. 330b, transition is made by a play on the double meaning of ποῖος. Compare Laws 655a where a play on the double meaning of χρῶμα serves as the transition to a slight digression. See also Phil. 14b; Rep 504bc.

[51] See Theaet. 176b.

Char. 157a where the sequence runs θεραπεύειν, θεραπεύεσθαι ἐπῳδαῖς, ἐπῳδὰς—λόγους, λόγων—ἐγγίγνεσθαι, ἐγγενομένης.

It would be easy to multiply examples of transition by repetition.[52] Those described will perhaps suffice to illustrate the possibilities of a simple mechanical device in the hands of a master.

In a form of literary expression like the philosophical dialogue special problems of transition confront the writer. The stream of question and answer must flow naturally and smoothly without becoming monotonous. Important points must be duly emphasized, minor details subordinated, necessary explanations introduced in such a way that they will not seem forced. In a general way all the methods of transition described above, the use of image, proverb, quotation and repeated word, contribute to the solution of these problems, for they add variety and interest. But these devices are not peculiar to the dialogue; they are equally suited to other forms of discourse. To meet more directly the special difficulties of the dialogue form, Plato employs transitions of another type which may be described as rhetorical methods for varying the conventional conduct of an argument. These more unusual forms of transition, however apparent their purpose may be to the student of literary style, seldom seem forced or artificial, but fit naturally into the logical framework of the dialogue. One such device has already been mentioned, the use of unusual or poetic words to surprise the attention and provoke inquiry for explanation. Plato makes use of paradox for a similar purpose.[53] The case may be very slight as in Rep. 377a where the paradoxical suggestion of the use of ψευδεῖς λόγοι in education requires explanation. Compare also Rep. 376ab where Socrates confirms the principle that the guardians must be lovers of wisdom by developing the analogy of the well-bred dog with the humorously paradoxical claim that the dog is fond of learning.

Without having recourse to actual paradox, Plato may state his idea in a figurative or elliptical way which is at first blush quite unintelligible; or he may use expressions intentionally difficult, obscure or

---

[52] See Theaet. 155cd, 156a, 158b–d, 172cd, 195bc; Protag. 361d; Symp. 178c; Euthyph. 3e; Laws 692d; Phaedr. 258de; Phaedo 72a, 92d, 109a; Phil. 19a, 28c, 29ab; Rep. 440cd, 504d, 548c, 607c, 608c. See Mendell, C. W., *Latin Sentence Connection*, pp. 21–85 for a complete treatment of the element of repetition in transition.

[53] See Phaedo 64; Rep. 422a. Also Phaedo 61bc and p. 6, n. 12.

technical. In all these cases it is the interlocutor's failure to understand which supplies the final step in transition to further explanation. So in Gorg. 463d Socrates' definition of rhetoric as a "shadow of a part of the political art" is purposely enigmatical and naturally provokes the demand for the long explanation which follows.[54] In Euthyphro 10a, the intellectually sluggish Euthyphro fails to grasp the significance of the distinction between essence and attribute implied in Socrates' question, whether the "holy is loved by the gods because it is holy, or holy because it is loved by the gods." His admission of his inability leads at once to more simple and detailed explanation. If the case of the slow-witted Euthyphro were the only one to be considered we might conclude that this "failure to understand" was introduced for the characterization of the respondent. But the fact that it is just as liable to be used of those who are quick in comprehension, like Theaetetus or Glaucon and Adeimantus, excludes such a theory; and the frequency of its occurrence[55] supports the view that it is purely transitional.

A variant on this method of transition is the respondent's ignorance of some point or his inability to grapple with some question.[56] This always shifts the burden of responsibility to Socrates. Thus in Phil. 48d Protarchus' inability to apply the method of diaeresis to the idea of ignorance of self, forces Socrates to undertake the task. So also in Theaet. 201d, Theaetetus' unwillingness to undertake to recall all the account which he has heard of "things knowable" paves the way for Socrates' long exposition. The respondent's misunderstanding[57] of some statement may serve as the excuse for further explanation. In Rep. 475d Glaucon's misinterpretation of Socrates' definition of the philosopher and his continued failure to understand the explanation by which Socrates narrows that definition lead to an interesting statement of the theory of ideas.

Similarly the respondent may himself advance a wrong but plausible view which comes under discussion thereby.[58] So in Rep. 439e

[54] See also Rep. 449c and pp. 39 f.

[55] Rep. 352e, 398c, 429c, 438b, 504d; Theaet. 152d, 155d, 164cd; Symp. 206b; Meno 81e; Phil. 26c, 44b, 51b; Phaedo 93a; Laws 700a, 960c. This method of transition may be repeated several times in the course of an exposition. See Theaet. 192c; Rep. 392c.

[56] See Theaet. 197a; Phil. 54b, 57b, 28b.

[57] See Phil. 14d; Rep. 523b.

[58] Phil. 21a; Rep. 578b.

Glaucon advances the opinion that the θυμός, instead of being a third element in the soul, may be akin to desire. This theory is thus in a natural manner brought up for consideration and refutation. The mistake of Cleinias in Laws 792b serves as the transition to an ethical discourse on pleasure and pain in the vein of the Philebus. In Laws 857bc, the dialogue is diversified by the error of the legislator in proposing an unreasonable law. He is recalled by Cleinias and the correction leads to a further discussion of the subject of proemia.

Self-correction is a similar device introduced into the argument for transitional purposes.[59] In Laws 894d the legislator corrects his own error in assigning the tenth place instead of the first to that motion which changes both itself and other things. He thereby emphasizes the importance of spontaneous motion. Similarly in Theaet. 195b–c Socrates' ironical[60] self-criticism introduces his discovery of an objection to his previous conclusion; the image of the wax-tablet does not explain all cases of false opinion.

The self-check[61] is a transitional device familiar to writers from Homer down.[62] In Plato it is sometimes playful or ironical in tone. So in Phaedrus 238c–d where Socrates pauses in the midst of his discourse on love to comment on his own inspired, dithyrambic style. Crat. 428d is very similar in tone. Socrates replies to the playfully extravagant praise of Cratylus, "I have long been wondering at my own wisdom; I cannot trust myself. And I think that I ought to stop and ask myself, what am I saying?" The self-check in this case forms the transition to a careful examination of the previous argument. In Phaedrus 260d Socrates checks himself in his criticism of rhetoric, "But perhaps, my friend, we have been abusing rhetoric more roughly than we ought." Thus the defence of rhetoric is introduced.

The type of transition in which a general expression of praise, satisfaction or assent is followed by the statement of "one little

---

[59] See Lysis 214e; Phil. 43b–c; Theaet. 169e.
[60] Note the repetition of the significant ἀδολέσχης.
[61] See Rep. 536b; Laws 701c, 722d, 803bc.
[62] ἀλλὰ τίη μοι ταῦτα φίλος διελέξατο θυμός; is a Homeric tag used in transition in soliloquy. Cf. Il. 22:121 and 385. Pindar, P. 4, 247 affords a striking example of the self-check in transition. See also P. 11, 38. For a less happy use of this transitional device see Apol. Rhod. I, 648 and 919.

difficulty" may be styled a literary variant of the dismissive-introductive transition. Protag. 328e–329b is a good example of this form of transition. Socrates dismisses with extravagant praise the myth of Protagoras just completed. "Yet," he concludes, "I have still one little difficulty." In this way the discussion of the unity of virtue is introduced.[63] Similarly, in Euthyphro 12e–13a these words of Socrates, "That is fine, Euthyphro, but there is still a little point on which I need further information," serve as the transition to investigation of the meaning of the term attention.

The dismissive expression of praise may be followed by an abrupt turn to a new point. This is the form which the transition takes when Socrates is baffled in the line of argument he has been pursuing.[64] So in Theaet. 163c "Splendid, Theaetetus, and it isn't worth while disputing with you about these matters, . . . but consider now this other difficulty which is coming up, and see how we shall get rid of it."

One of the most characteristic devices for introducing a discussion is the Socratic profession of ignorance.[65] "You perhaps understand, Polemarchus, but I do not." These half ironical words of Socrates preface the testing of the definition of justice supported by the authority of Simonides, Rep. 331e. So in the beginning of the Meno (71b), Meno asks Socrates whether virtue can be taught. After a complimentary contrast between the flourishing condition of wisdom in Thessaly and the drought in Athens, Socrates introduces the discussion by a very emphatic avowal of his own ignorance: "Now I myself, Meno, am in like case; I share my fellow citizens' poverty in this respect; and I blame myself for knowing nothing at all about virtue; and when I do not know what a thing is, how could I know anything about its characteristics?" By the cleverly inserted distinction between essence and attribute the subject of discussion is shifted to 'what is virtue.'

The imaginary or supposed question in its different forms affords an easy method of varying the transitions from point to point in a

---

[63] For further examples see Theaet. 145d, 161c, 202d; Char. 154e; Symp. 201c; Laches 180b. Less clearly marked cases occur in Protag. 319ab; Euthyph. 7a; Phaedo 69e.

[64] In Protag. 351b the new point is introduced abruptly without connection with the preceding through any expression of satisfaction.

[65] For other examples see Meno 80cd; Laches 186c; Theaet. 145e, 157cd; Rep. 354c, 450e–451ab; Gorg. 506a; Lysis 212a; Crat. 384c.

discussion. It may be little more than a softened form of inquiry used for politeness' sake. Compare Meno 72b where the question really adds nothing to the transition except the artistic effect of a varied phraseology.[66] An imagined request for explanation on the part of the respondent may introduce the concrete illustration of some point, or the description of an analogous case. So in Rep. 337a and 341e. Or the questioner and respondent may be represented as being interrogated by an imaginary third party.[67] This is the form most frequently used by Plato. So in Protag. 353a seq. Socrates sets forth the meaning of the phrase, "being overcome by pleasure," and the theory of the balancing of pains and pleasures, by means of a long imaginary dialogue with οἱ πολλοὶ τῶν ἀνθρώπων. Various formulas introduce these questions and serve as the explicit verbal transition in each case.

While the invented interlocutor is usually the versatile and ever-present τις he sometimes assumes a more definite character as in Theaet. 200ab; "For that hero of dialectic will say with a laugh." Here an objection is dramatically put in the mouth of an imaginary eristic opponent who is mentioned also in 197a and 165d. In 165d the description of the experience of Theaetetus at the hands of this imaginary eristic questioner leads to a return to the subject of the defence of Protagoras, mentioned already in 164e. In this defence, Socrates imagines Protagoras himself addressing them. This is the final stage in the development of the device of an imaginary interlocutor.[68]

The reported imaginary conversation of a man with himself is another transitional device employed for the sake of variety. So in Phil. 38c–d Socrates introduces and develops a psychological analysis of perception and recognition by describing the imaginary discourse of the mind with itself. τις merely takes the place of ἡμᾶς in this passage. Again, in Euthyphro 9c, Socrates sets forth in dramatic form as an imaginary discourse with himself his doubts whether he has yet learned from Euthyphro the nature of piety. This leads to an assumption for the sake of argument that Euthyphro may be

---

[66] See also Symp. 199e.

[67] See Symp. 204d; Gorg. 451ab; Protag. 311b, c, de, 312d, 330c, d, e, 331a; Rep. 332c; Theaet. 147a, 163d, 184b, 188d, 195c, 203a, et al.

[68] See also Theaet. 154c, 178b; Phaedr. 268a–e, 269a–c.

right in his claims in regard to the impiety of his father's act, and so to a further demand for the definition of piety.

Transition may be made by the interlocutor's answering his own question or anticipating and forestalling an objection.[69] In Protag. 325c, Protagoras' answer to his own rhetorical question introduces his account of Greek education. In Laws 893a, the legislator's stated intention to answer his own questions and avoid bewildering his companions, forms one element in the highly figurative transition to the proof that soul is prior to body. Throughout the enumeration of the ten kinds of motion the legislator follows this method. In Gorg. 505cd this method is employed under slightly different circumstances. Callicles refuses to continue the discussion with Socrates and remains firm in his decision in spite of Socrates' plea that the argument shall not be left without a head. When Socrates asks for a volunteer to help him finish the debate, Callicles suggests the possibility that he himself assume the rôle of respondent to his own questions. With the approval of the others Socrates adopts this plan and for some time continues the discussion alone except for an occasional appeal to Callicles for his approval. By 510a, however, Callicles has been insensibly won over to good nature and is again drawn into the argument.[70]

When discussion is blocked, the sudden recollection of some forgotten words of another may effect the transition to a new definition or further argument.[71] In Theaet. 201c, the conclusion has been reached that knowledge and true opinion are not identical. Transition is made to the new definition of knowledge as true opinion μετὰ λόγου by the words of Theaetetus, "I had forgotten, Socrates; that is just what I have heard from some one else; and now I recall it."[72] And Socrates, in introducing his discussion of this definition, picks up the words of Theaetetus with the colloquial phrase, "Hear

---

[69] Compare Symp. 208d; Euthyph. 7cd.

[70] There is a similar situation in the Protagoras. In 360d, Protagoras sees his refutation inevitable and refuses to answer. When pressed by Socrates, he retorts "Finish it yourself." Here, however, there is no transition to further discussion. Socrates extorts one last admission from the reluctant sophist and then passes to defence of his own purpose and general remarks on the outcome of the discussion.

[71] Cf. Phil. 20b; Phaedr. 259e; Char. 161b; Lysis 215c.

[72] Note that γέ meaning "to-wit" picks up ἄλλο of the previous conclusion, thus aiding in the transition.

then a dream in return for a dream," and declares that he too is not speaking upon his own authority.

In the Meno (80e–81a), when further discussion seems blocked by Meno's introduction of the sophistic argument about the impossibility of inquiry, Socrates introduces his eloquent, poetical exposition of the theory of recollection with the statement that he has heard it "from certain wise men and women who spoke of things divine." But the reference to other authority is unconnected here with any hint of forgetfulness or sudden remembrance. Again in the Phaedrus (235b) this same idea, the recollection of some words of the wise, is an important element in the transition to Socrates' extravagant speech in favor of the non-lover. Phaedrus has finished reading aloud the speech of Lysias and demands Socrates' opinion of it. When Socrates ventures upon some criticism, Phaedrus protests. But Socrates persists in his opinion. He recalls that he has heard "ancient sages, men and women, who have spoken and written of these things." And he is sure that, repeating what he has heard, he can make "a speech as good as that of Lysias and different." With characteristic Socratic irony he protests that the speech is no invention of his own, though he cannot remember at the moment from whom he heard it.[73]

The transition by a protest or apology, common in the orators[74] is found also in Plato. "Then I must speak," says Glaucon in Rep. 361e, "and now if my language is rather coarse, Socrates, please to suppose that it is not I who speak, but those who praise injustice instead of justice." With this disclaimer of responsibility, Glaucon prefaces the second part of his defence of the unjust life. So in Gorg. 494e, Socrates prefaces his demand whether Callicles still maintains that pleasure and good are identical by a protest that Callicles is to blame for the coarse tone of the preceding argument.[75]

---

[73] In the two passages last described this transition also marks the change to a more elevated style. It is interesting to compare the transitions in Rep. 614b; Gorg. 522e–523a; Phaedo 110b.

[74] Orators often introduce a statement or a line of argument with the apologetic protest that their opponents force them to take this position—e.g., Dem. XVIII, 228, 269, 312; Isoc. XV, 310; Lysias III, 3; XII, 3; Isaeus II, 1.

[75] See also Phaedr. 237a. Socrates' protest in Rep. 509c that Glaucon is to blame for any exaggeration, "for you made me utter my fancies," is not strictly speaking transitional, though it is picked up by Glaucon in his demand that the discussion be continued. Rather it is a bit of by-play introduced to relieve the strain caused by the long, difficult argument.

For the sake of variety Plato sometimes plays with the order and plan of the subject.[76] Such a structural device is necessarily transitional, since it offers a means of introducing topics effectively and of regulating discussion. The frequent comparison of the argument to a wind which must be followed whithersoever it blows, is not of course to be taken seriously.[77] "Such words," says Campbell,[78] "express the spirit of the catechetical mode of expression, but only a blind simplicity can believe the master serious when he professes not to know the way." Whenever Plato plays with the order of his subject, it is for artistic reasons and not because the plan was not firmly fixed in his own mind. In Rep. 430d, after the discussion of courage, Socrates pretends to want to pass on to justice at once "without any longer troubling ourselves about temperance." Adeimantus protests. By this dramatic by-play, the transition to the definition of temperance is varied. Similarly, in Rep. 457e, instead of turning directly to the discussion of the desirability of the second paradox, the community of wives, Socrates attempts to escape by the assumption that its advantages are self-evident if only it is possible. Glaucon, however, will not permit this evasion, and the discussion thus introduced proceeds.

Frequently, the leader of the discussion pretends to have stumbled on a point, when in reality he has led up to it through a carefully prepared image or argument. So, in Laws 722cd, the analogy of the slave physician and the true has prepared the way for the principle that all laws need a preamble. This idea of the necessity of a preamble and the conclusion that all their previous words have been in reality naught but prelude are nevertheless introduced as unforeseen and due to lucky chance.

Again in Laws 888, the long discussion of the difficulties of meeting the problem of religious scepticism really forms a very fitting introduction to the following generalization of the pre-Socratic nature philosophy; the Athenian stranger, however, exclaims at the remarkable discussion into which they have unwittingly fallen (Laws 888d).[79]

[76] Although this method of variation is especially characteristic of the Republic and Laws, it is not confined to these dialogues. Compare Theaet. 183b–184b; Symp. 185c–e.
[77] See Introduction, p. 1.
[78] Essays in Edition of Rep., Vol. II, p. 10.
[79] Cf. also Rep. 399e; Laws 681c, 686c.

In the Republic and Laws, it is usually comparatively easy to distinguish the literary machinery from the real argument. This is not always the case. One of the most important features of Platonic style and one that has often misled critics, is his playful blending of real arguments with mere literary devices for carrying out an illustrative imagery.[80] The concluding pages of the Philebus perhaps afford the most considerable example of this puzzling confusion. In 59c–d Socrates has really established his thesis, the superiority of knowledge over pleasure.[81] Further confirmation is not needed except for rhetorical effect. In 59d–e a dismissive εἶεν and an image derived from the idea of the μικτόν introduce a summary of previous arguments. A proverb[82] serves as the final step in transition to this résumé. A challenge to other investigators (60d) prefaces the restatement (61ab) of their earlier[83] conclusion that neither knowledge nor pleasure unmixed is the good; the good is in the mixed life where it dwells as a man in his home. Various images and literary conceits follow, carrying out the figure of the mixture and serving as a transition to the piece of serious reasoning that follows. "In the life that is well mixed" the good will appear more clearly. Let us pray to the gods and make the mixture. We are like wine mixers; pleasure is like honey; knowledge like water. Finally, with φέρε δή and the picking up of καλῶς, Socrates turns (61d) to the serious question whether every form of pleasure and knowledge should be admitted to the mixture. Knowledge is considered first and in 62bc the conclusion is established that all forms of knowledge, even the imperfect, will be necessary. The following images of the porter opening wide the door, and of the receiving basin of streams emphasize and develop this conclusion in figurative language. In the second image, Plato finds a suggestion for his transition to the consideration of pleasure; "And now we must go back to the fountain of pleasures" (62d). "It is time now for us to consider about the pleasures too, whether we must let in all these together also" (62e). True and necessary pleasures will of course be admitted. With regard to the other pleasures the previous course of the dialogue has shown Plato's opinion clearly enough. Accordingly, instead of repeating the argu-

[80] As in Rep. 375–6. See p. 80.
[81] See pp. 32 f.
[82] See p. 74.
[83] 22bc.

ment, he adopts the literary device of an imaginary dialogue with the pleasures and sciences themselves (63a–64a), asking their opinion on the subject of admitting all forms of pleasure. This gives him an opportunity to review the previous conclusions in a striking, dramatic way.

With an abrupt formula of transition, ἀλλὰ μὴν καὶ τόδε γὲ ἀναγκαῖον (64a), Plato now turns to the somewhat arbitrary selection of truth, symmetry and beauty as the three chief elements of good. The figure of the dwelling place of the good recurs (64c) and a figure from the chase emphasizes his conclusion (65a), "Then if we cannot hunt the good with one idea only, with three we may capture it." We are ready now for the triumphant final decision, "And now, Protarchus, any man could be an adequate judge for us concerning pleasure and wisdom, as to which of them is more akin to the highest good and more to be honored among men and gods." In the remainder of the dialogue, Plato is merely adding further reasons in a somewhat rhetorical style, in order to make his conclusion more effective. The words of Protarchus (65b) show this, "That is plain, nevertheless at any rate it is better to go through with the argument." The distinctions and terms of these last pages should not, therefore, be too closely pressed. Bury[84] and Poste make this mistake when they criticize the argument which identifies truth with mind rather than with pleasure, because Plato refers to pleasures of love instead of pure pleasures. This is all mere rhetorical reinforcement of the argument; his conclusion has already been established.

Through a similar error, too much is often made of the six grades enumerated in 66. They are not to be taken seriously. They are aptly introduced by a playfully exaggerated command to Protarchus to proclaim their decision far and wide,[85] and end in a quotation which is also a figure, "And now, with the sixth generation, as Orpheus says, cease the glory of my song" (66c). In transition καταπαύσατε is picked up by καταπεπαυμένος. The following figure of putting a head on the argument and the proverbial "third to the savior" introduce a third and final[86] restatement both of the original thesis and the question of the second prize and a third and final résumé of their conclusions. Socrates closes with the triumphant boast that we shall not

---

[84] Bury, *Philebus*, Appendix B, p. 169 ff.
[85] The transition in Rep. 580b is similar in tone. Cf. p. 44.
[86] Cf. 19c, 60a.

believe pleasure to be first in importance even if all men and beasts so affirm. Although the exposition is complete, the dialogue ends with Protarchus still unwilling to let Socrates go, a touch probably added by Plato to heighten the resemblance of the Philebus in outward form to the minor dialogues of search.

In the passage just analyzed it is significant to note that it is only after his thesis is established that Plato gives his fancy free rein. The resultant baffling mixture of rhetoric and serious thought does not effect his conclusions; there is no sacrifice of logical clearness for the sake of ornament. Another evidence of Plato's care in guarding against confusion in the argument is found in his treatment of digressions. An explicit warning does not usually precede the digression, but the resumption of the argument at its close is always clearly marked. The method of approach to a digression is naturally determined in great measure by its content and purpose. The digression may be a passage of by-play or of eloquent moral reflection which serves to vary the monotony and relieve the strain of a difficult argument; or it may be a discussion of some subject supplemental to, or illustrative of the main argument. Euthyphro 11b–e furnishes an example of the first type of digression. Euthyphro is completely at a loss and complains that their arguments "seem to turn around and walk away." The suggestion of motion leads Socrates into a comparison of their words to the handiwork of Daedalus. The playful discussion of the application of this metaphor affords a pleasant relief from the preceding subtle dialectic. The transition here is cleverly made through the development of a chance expression.[87] It is only at its close (11e) that the passage is marked as a digression by the explicit dismissal, "Enough of this," and the restatement of the question at issue, the nature of piety.[88]

It is entirely natural that the idea of leisure should frequently appear in transition to a digression. In the case of the charming poetical digression in Phaedrus 258e–259e it is introduced merely to justify the digression. But in Theaet. 172b it not only serves this purpose; it is also the chief element in the transition[89] to Socrates' long

---

[87] For digressions similarly introduced see Rep. 466d; Phil. 12bc, 28ab; Phaedr. 258e; Laws 692d.

[88] Compare Laws 655b where a slight digression on color is dismissed with the phrase "not to be tedious." Also Phil. 59b–c.

[89] See p. 24.

eloquent description of the life of the philosopher as contrasted with that of the clever, unscrupulous lawyer.[90] The return from this lengthy digression is marked by a dismissive apology (with μὲν οὖν). "These however," says Socrates, "are digressions from which we must now desist, or they will overflow and drown the original argument; to which, if you please, we will now return" (Theaet. 177bc). A careful resumptive summary of the argument follows (177c). Another slighter instance in which the dismissal takes the form of an explicit apologetic recognition that what precedes is a digression[91] is found in Rep. 571a–572b. This is a digression of the supplemental type.[92] The transition to it is rather abrupt. Before proceeding with the description of the tyrannical soul, Socrates brings up "a previous question which remains unanswered, . . . the nature and number of the appetites." He himself declares that until this subject is adequately treated, "the inquiry will always be confused." The supplemental character of the digression is thus explicitly recognized. At the close of this discussion Socrates remarks, "In saying this I have been running into a digression; but," he continues, resuming the argument, "the point which I desire to note is that in all of us, even in good men, there is a lawless wild-beast nature, which peers out in sleep."

More often the dismissal of the digression is not explicit, merely implied by a resumptive statement, or the repetition, with some resumptive particle, of the point under consideration before the digression.[93] So in Laws 693c the Athenian returns from an illustrative[94] digression (692d–693c) on the Persian Wars with the remark, "Let us resume the argument in that spirit," picking up the idea of the legislator's need of an ideal aim, a point which the digression has emphasized. Again in Protag. 328a–329b, Socrates' remark that he has "one little difficulty" is repeated, with νῦν δή, at the end of the

[90] For further examples of edifying moral or religious digressions cf. Phil. 28c–30e; Laws 803a seq.; Phaedo 89c–91c.

[91] For further examples of apologetic dismissal cf. Phil. 30e and Rep. 543c. For a full description of the latter passage see p. 42.

[92] Bks. V–VII of the Republic form a lengthy digression which supplements the argument. See discussion in Chap. I, pp. 39 f.

[93] Cf. Theaet. 151d, 165e.

[94] Further examples of this type of digression: Theaet. 165a–e; Laws 655ab; Rep. 466d–471a.

ironical digression in which he explains his confidence in Protagoras, and serves as the transition to renewed discussion.

Another interesting topic which should be at least touched upon in any study of Plato's literary methods of transition is his treatment of transition in parodies. The myth in the Protagoras, the speech of Lysias in the Phaedrus, the speech of Aspasia in the Menexenus and the speeches of Aristophanes, Agathon and the rest in the Symposium are the most considerable examples of parody in the dialogues. So cleverly has Plato imitated the manner of these other writers that there have not been lacking critics in modern times as well as in antiquity to maintain that the passages in question are not parody at all, but the authentic work of the authors to whom they are ascribed by Plato.[95] But the fact that, aside from these passages, Plato has shown himself able completely to vary his style at will establishes his ability to write parody; and it certainly seems far more probable that such an artist would exercise his own creative power rather than be limited by dependence on other writers. However, setting aside the question of Platonic authorship, it is interesting to note the methods of transition used in some of these passages, as they illustrate types of style quite different from the dramatic description, the continuous dialectic or the stichomythia of question and answer which make up a large part of the dialogues.

The myth in the Protagoras (320c seq.) is an example of simple narrative style. It opens with a narrative γάρ. The sentences are short. The methods of connection are uniformly simple; narrative conjunctions, such as ἐπειδή, ὅτι, ὅταν; transitional particles

---

[95] This view finds most general credence in the case of the speech of Lysias. Blass (*Attische Beredsamkeit*, Leipzig, 1887, Vol. I, pp. 423-430), while accepting the Platonic authorship of the speeches in the Symposium, maintains that the resemblance to the style of Lysias in the speech in the Phaedrus is too perfect to admit of its being parody. He lists the authorities ancient and modern on both sides of the question.

Adam in his edition of the Protagoras (pp. xxi-xxii, Cambridge, 1893) argues against the Platonic authorship of the myth. But his reasoning is defective. Intent to caricature is not the only adequate motive for parody; and it is unfair to base any arguments upon the disputed speech in Phaedrus 233 ff. Adam cites Zeller (*Archiv. für Geschichte der Philosophie*, V 2, p. 175 ff.) and Chiapelli (*ibid.* III, p. 15 and 256 f.) who support the same view. The ancient authorities are listed by Stallbaum (Ed. of Protagoras, Leipzig, 1882, p. 77). For the other view see Stewart (*Myths of Plato*, London, 1905, pp. 220-222), and Grote, (*Plato*, Vol. II, London, 1888, pp. 274-275).

μὲν-δέ, καί, γάρ, οὖν, δή, μὲν οὖν; deictic pronouns and adverbs, repeated words. The time sequence forms the chief bond of connection throughout.

The speech of Agathon (Symp. 194e–197e) is a brilliant rhetorical display in the sophistic style. The transitions are explicit. Each subject is formally announced and as formally dismissed. The speech opens with a prothetic statement of plan. πρῶτον μὲν and ἔπειτα introduce the two topics of the discourse; first, the method to be adopted in the praise of Eros; second, the actual encomium. The rhetorical balance is further continued through the contrast of the wrong methods of previous speakers with that to be used by Agathon. The summarizing application concluding this brief discussion of method is introduced by οὕτω δή (195a). πρῶτον and ἔπειτα again appear in enumeration. A transitional οὖν introduces the first point in the encomium; Eros is the most blessed of the gods because he is the fairest and best. The proofs of his preeminent beauty are discussed first. πρῶτον μὲν introduces the first point, his youth. When this is established, advance to the next is made through the common dismissive-introductive form of transition with μὲν οὖν and δέ (195c). A dismissal of these two points (with μὲν δή) combined with the introductory phrase πρὸς δὲ τούτοις (196a) marks the transition to the third. Another explicit transition of the formal dismissive-introductive type effects the advance from the subject of the beauty of Eros to that of his virtue. This theme likewise is treated with rhetorical formality. The four virtues are considered in turn. The following phrases mark the transitions; τὸ μὲν μέγιστον (196b) introduces the claim that Eros is just; πρὸς δὲ τῇ δικαιοσύνῃ σωφροσύνης πλείστης μετέχει (196c) marks the advance to temperance; with καὶ μήν the encomiast proceeds to the subject of courage. These three are now formally dismissed with μὲν οὖν and the remaining virtue, wisdom, is presented for consideration by a common introductive formula (196d). Throughout the speech the more minute transitions in the discussion of the various points are also explicit. Proofs are carefully labelled as such (195b, d; 196a). A summarizing οὕτως and the common adverbial phrase μετὰ τοῦτο mark the transition (197c) to the final topic, Eros' benefits to men. The eloquent Gorgian conclusion is the most notable parody of the flamboyant style and displays to perfection its chief features, antithesis, balance, alliteration, assonance, homoeoteleuton, jingling word-play, exaggeration, asyndeton. For its unity this passage depends upon word-order and rhythm.

The much debated Menexenus[96] is another and even more striking instance of Plato's parody[97] of the epideictic style, in this case the ἐπιτάφιος. Its subject matter deals with the regular τόποι of this class of literature.[98] The style is balanced and rhetorical and employs transitional methods similar to those just described. For example in 236d note the transitional use of the favorite rhetorical antithesis between word and deed and the studied balance of phrases. There is the same formal statement of theme and summarizing dismissal of conclusions, the same constant use of rhetorical figures that were noted in Symp. 194e–197e.

The much-disputed speech of Lysias in the Phaedrus illustrates the plain rhetorical manner. Aside from the continual use of balance few figures of style appear. The methods of connection are simple, even monotonous;[99] a few particles, used over and over, form practically the entire machinery of transition. The balance with μέν and δέ occurs repeatedly, the balance ἀλλά—οὐ eight times in 233 and 234. ἔτι δέ is used four times (231a, b, 232a, 233d), καὶ μὲν δή five times (231d, 232b, e, 233a, d). The frequent use of the conjunction ὥστε should also be noted.

[96] Burgess, *Epideictic Literature*, University of Chicago Press, 1902, p. 148, note 1, cites the literature on the genuineness of the dialogue.

[97] That the Menexenus is avowedly a parody seems clear from the conclusion (249de) where Menexenus plainly hints at his disbelief in Aspasia's authorship.

[98] Burgess, *op. cit.*, pp. 146-157, analyzes the content of the Menexenus and compares it with the other extant examples of ἐπιτάφιοι.

[99] Blass has noted this (p. 430 note).

APPENDIX

Although this study of Plato's methods of transition is by no means statistically complete, yet the amount of material collected will justify a few general conclusions as to variations in usage in earlier and later dialogues. Chronologically the Platonic dialogues may be divided into three main groups. The minor Socratic dialogues are generally regarded as early; the Theaetetus and Republic are typical of the middle period; while the Laws, Timaeus and difficult metaphysical and dialectical dialogues are undoubtedly late.[1]

In the later dialogues the frame-work is obvious. The transitions are usually explicit. Formal detailed statements of method, prescribing the course to be followed or the principles which are to govern the discussion, and summarizing résumés are naturally characteristic of these difficult dialogues. The frequent occurrence of these types of transition in the Laws and Philebus has been noted.[2]

In the dialogues of the middle period the bald outlines of the plot are disguised under a wealth of imagery and dramatic detail. Transitional summaries and statements of plan occur, but they are less prominent and are often combined with other elements.[3] The more artistic and unusual forms of transition discussed in chapter three occur with greatest frequency in the dialogues of the middle period.

The minor dialogues of search illustrate most clearly the pretence at lack of plan which is a chracteristic feature of Platonic method. Transitional references to the course of the argument are generally brief and simple; if at all lengthy they are embellished by dramatic

---

[1] Minute statistical investigation of Plato's style, diction and use of particles have contributed materially to the solution of the problem of dating the dialogues. But such evidence, however valuable for confirming the general classification of a dialogue as early, middle or late, must not be regarded as alone sufficient to date a dialogue. Cf. Shorey, *Unity*, pp. 49 ff. The most important of these statistical studies are—C. Ritter, *Untersuchungen*, Stuttgartt, 1888; Campbell, Introduction to Edition of Sophist and Politicus, Oxford Press, 1867; Campbell, Essays I and III in Vol. II of Jowett and Campbell's *Republic*, Oxford Press, 1894; W. Dittenberger—τί μήν; (*Hermes*, Vol. XVI, 1881, pp. 321-345); Schanz—τῷ ὄντι and ὄντως (*Hermes*, Vol. XXI, 1886).

[2] Cf. Chap. II, p. 56, also Chap. I, pp. 26, 47.

[3] Cf. Theaet. 191a–c, 187d–e.

and artistic details.[4] Conventional transitional formulas and phrases occur in great numbers in all the dialogues. They are indeed essential to the catechetical form. Statistical study, however, reveals the tendency to a decided increase in their use in the dialogues of the middle period, while their excessive occurrence in the later dialogues contributes largely to bring about that greater formality and artificiality of style which has been noted by scholars.[5] The transitional usage, in typical dialogues, of forms of ποῖος will illustrate this point. In the Laches, Lysis and Charmides, which are presumably early, there are only three instances of forms of ποῖος in transition, once in the common formula τὸ ποῖον δὴ τοῦτο and twice in oblique cases, ποίῳ and ποίαν. In the Theaetetus the number of cases is increased to thirteen, all stereotyped phrases with ποῖον or ποῖα. But in the Philebus, which is late, ποῖον and ποῖα occur in transition forty-three times. Similar statistics might be gathered on the transitional usage of πῶς, λέγε μόνον, and other stereotyped transitional phrases.

[4] Cf. Laches 190c–d, 197e; Lysis 213e.
[5] Campbell, *Republic*, Vol. II, pp. 60-61.

INDEX OF REFERENCES TO THE PLATONIC DIALOGUES

(Numbers refer to pages of the dissertation. Mere lists of passages in foot-notes are not included.)

Charmides, 6, 7, 8, 10, 13, 14, 16, 54, 74, 75, 86, 103.
Cratylus, 4, 13, 54, 74, 76, 89.
Crito, 8.
Euthydemus, 11, 73.
Euthyphro, 6, 7, 13, 54, 59, 62, 85, 86, 88, 90, 91, 97.
Gorgias, 9, 15, 17, 18, 54, 60, 74, 75, 76, 84, 88, 92, 93.
Laches, 6, 7, 8, 14, 16, 17, 54, 56, 58, 59, 64, 66, 73, 78, 79, 80, 86, 103.
Laws, 47–52, 55, 58, 60, 64, 75, 80, 83, 86, 89, 92, 94, 98, 102.
Lysis, 5, 13, 16, 72, 103.
Menexenus, 101.
Meno, 5, 13, 18, 19, 55, 60, 61, 63, 76, 80, 84, 85, 90, 91, 93.
Parmenides, 5, 13.
Phaedo, 6, 11, 15, 16, 19–22, 73, 81, 85, 98.
Phaedrus, 9, 15, 18, 21, 56, 71, 74, 79, 89, 93, 97, 101.
Philebus, 5, 26–33, 58, 59, 63, 69, 74, 75, 76, 83, 88, 91, 95–97, 102, 103.
Politicus, 5, 13, 74, 83.
Protagoras, 6, 10, 11, 14, 17, 54, 55, 56, 57, 58, 62, 63, 64, 65, 75, 86, 90, 91, 92, 98, 99,
Republic, 12, 15, 21, 33–47, 56, 57, 58, 62, 63, 72, 73, 74, 75, 76, 77, 78, 79, 80, 81, 82, 84, 85, 87, 88, 90, 91, 93, 94, 98, 102.
Sophist, 4, 13, 74.
Spurious Dialogues, 5.
Symposium, 10, 12, 14, 21, 71, 76, 77, 78, 79, 84, 100.
Theaetetus, 12, 13, 21, 22–26, 54, 55, 57, 60, 62, 64, 69, 74, 77, 78, 79, 82, 83, 85, 86, 88, 89, 90, 91, 92, 97, 98, 102, 103.
Timaeus, 102.

ANCIENT PHILOSOPHY

1. Otto Apelt. *Platonis Sophista. Recensuit, Prolegomenis et Commentariis Instruxit*
2. Grace Hadley Billings. *The Art of Transition in Plato*
3. Thomas H. Billings. *The Platonism of Philo Judaeus*
4. Ingram Bywater. *Aristotle on the Art of Poetry. A Revised Text with Critical Introduction and Commentary.*
5. Lewis Campbell. *The Theaetetus of Plato. A Revised Text and English Notes.* Second Edition
6. Henri Carteron. *La notion de force dans le système d'Aristote*
7. Harold Cherniss. *The Riddle of the Early Academy*
8. Ingemar Düring. *Aristotle's De Partibus Animalium. Critical and Literary Commentaries*
9. Ingemar Düring. *Aristotle's Chemical Treatise. Meterologica, Book IV. With an introduction and commentary*
10. Ingemar Düring. *Die Harmonienlehre des Klaudios Ptolemaios* bound with Ingemar Düring. *Porphyrios Kommentar zur Harmonienlehre des Ptolemaios*
11. Ingemar Düring. *Ptolemaios und Porphyrios über die Musik*
12. Wilmer Cave France. *The Emperor Julian's Relation to the New Sophistic and Neo-Platonism: with a study of his style*
13. John Gibb and William Montgomery. *The Confessions of Augustine.* Second Edition

14. Carlo Giussani. *T. Lucreti Cari De Rerum Natura Libri Sex. Revisione del testo, commento e studi introduttivi*
15. Sir Thomas Heath. *Mathematics in Aristotle*
16. William A. Heidel. *Selected Papers*. Edited with an introduction by Leonardo Tarán
17. Roger Miller Jones. *The Platonism of Plutarch and Selected Papers*. Edited with an introduction by Leonardo Tarán
18. Hal Koch. *Pronoia und Paideusis. Studien über Origenes und sein Verhältnis zum Platonismus*
19. Clara Elizabeth Millerd. *On the Interpretation of Empedocles*
20. Constantin Ritter. *Bibliographies on Plato* ("Berichte . . . über Platon erschienenen Arbeiten")
21. Léon Robin. *Pyrrhon et le scepticisme grec*
22. Richard Robinson. *Plato's Earlier Dialectic.* Second Edition
23. W.D. Ross. *Aristotle's Prior and Posterior Analytics. A Revised Text with Introduction and Commentary*
24. Paul Shorey. *Selected Papers.* Edited with an introduction by Leonardo Tarán
25. Paul Shorey. *The Unity of Plato's Thought*
26. G. Stallbaum. *Platonis Opera Omnia.* (This set is published here in fourteen volumes and includes Stallbaum's commentary on Plato's *Parmenides*.)
27. E. Seymer Thompson. *The Meno of Plato, edited with Introduction, Notes, and Excursuses*
28. Eliza Gregory Wilkins. *"Know Thyself" in Greek and Latin Literature*
29. John Cook Wilson. *On the Interpretation of Plato's Timaeus. Critical studies with reference to a recent edition*
    bound with
    John Cook Wilson. *"On the Platonist Doctrine of the ἀσύμβλητοι ἀριθμοί"*